Smart Teenage Muslimah

An inspirational guide for Muslim girls

Farhat Amin

Smart Teenage Muslimah

By Farhat Amin

www.smartmuslima.com

Want Free Bonus Content?

Scan Me Now!

CONTENTS

INTRODUCTION

Bismillah ar-Rahman, ar-Rahim, I begin in the name of Allah, the Beneficent, the Merciful. All praises and thanks to the One Who created us with a mind capable of understanding and acting on His divine guidance. Mubarak on selecting such an excellent book; maybe your mum or another relative gifted it to you. Regardless of how it got to you, I hope you enjoy every page of this book, even the ones you find a little daunting.

As you know better than me, Muslim teenagers face unique challenges. A myth is peddled that following Islam makes your life difficult, and you'll be happier if you were less religious. Similar struggles to yours were experienced by the young men described in Surah Kahf. They were under immense pressure to abandon their deen and follow social norms. What did they do about it? They escaped so they would not have compromise their faith. Allah protected them, and they slept for over three hundred years in the cave. Alhamdulillah, they were never discovered.

When they awoke, they felt like they had only slept for a little while. One of them went to buy food, hoping the enemy wouldn't capture him. But the locals noticed he had coins and clothing from three centuries ago. Allah had saved the young men from their oppressors, who had passed away, and the town was now full of believers.

Let's face it, sometimes being a practising Muslim can seem like Mission Impossible. Sin is fashionable: Islam is outdated. The boys could have abandoned their belief in tawhid, but their trust in Allah was greater than their fear. Surah Kahf teaches us that when we hold on to Islam, Allah will protect us, even allowing us time travel![1]

So, rather than blame Islam for your problems, I want to offer a new point of view. Firstly, I invite you to look at the ideas and behaviours that wider society expects you to embrace and decide whether they are good for your mental health and well-being. Concepts such as self-obsession, rampant consumerism and feminism. Secondly, what tools exist in the Quran and Sunnah to help you dream big, be a confident Muslimah and achieve peace of mind?

I want you to know that being a Muslim is the best thing in the world. You are truly blessed! Don't listen to anyone who tells you otherwise. Imagine being unaware that Allah created you. Or worse, being taught to worship idols? Or that you evolved from apes?

Inshallah, I hope to provide clear answers to fundamental questions, such as why you should believe in Allah and what is the miracle of the Quran. Your belief in Islam must be built on a solid foundation so that you can flourish in this life and the next. That way, as you travel through life, your rule book (Quran and Sunnah) will not be replaced by a 'do whatever feels good' mantra.

I was a high school teacher, so I am conscious of the demands placed on you. I've seen my students, family, and friends struggle with maintaining their Islamic identity while also trying to fit in.

Why did I write this book? The inspiration for this book comes from Surah Asr, 103: *'By Time. The human being is in loss. Except those who believe, and do good works, and encourage truth, and recommend patience.'* The advice I offer you genuinely comes from a place of love. We don't know each other, but we are sisters, connected by our belief in Allah and His Messenger (saw). I am in no position to judge you.

I made a tonne of mistakes when I was growing up, and in the pages of this book, I want to share what I have discovered through those experiences. In addition, I enjoy digging into the 'Why' behind the cultural shifts that Muslim women are experiencing. Why are young Muslims led to believe that life would be better if they didn't obey their Creator?

There's so much toxic competitiveness when you're a teenage girl; are my thighs smaller than hers? Am I prettier? Do boys like me more? Social media adds to the pressure, and society tells young women they must look sexy and act sexy. I'm fascinated by the topic and want to show you how Islam can help you resolve your problems.

Together let's explore issues you have to deal with, like body image, puberty, gender relations and feminism. This is the book I wish I had when I was a teenager to help me make sense of complicated topics. You are at the start of your life's journey, a journey that can be the most incredible thing.

Please note that this is not a comprehensive book of fiqh or legal rulings relating to Muslimahs; however, it is based on the teachings of the Quran and the Sunnah. Numerous excellent Islamic resources explain the rights and responsibilities of young Muslimahs in Islam. Please access them to understand these rules better and read about the life of the Prophet (saw), so you know how to live a god-conscious life. This book primarily addresses contemporary challenges confronting teenage Muslimahs in the twenty-first century.

The Quran's references are provided in the following format: (Al-Baqara, 2:3) refers to the third verse in chapter two of the Quran. References to hadith indicate the collection of hadith (Muslim, Bukhari, Tirmidhi, etc.)

A few chapters, such as 'Feminism explained', are pretty in-depth because I had to explain the history of feminism to help you truly grasp the subject. Additionally, I've provided a glossary to help you understand unfamiliar terms and a reference list so you can fact-check the sources I use in the book. The book also includes two poems from the incredibly gifted poet Zaynab Mufti.

So, if you're a 'Smart Teenage Muslimah' whose goal is to succeed in this life and attain jannah in the next: this book is for you. If you have any questions you can connect with me via my website. Inshallah, let's remember each other in our duas.

Your sister Farhat Amin
www.smartmuslima.com

WHY YOU SHOULD BELIEVE IN ALLAH

Wouldn't it be great if someone would simply demonstrate Allah's existence? No telling off. No drama. No statements like 'You have to believe!' So, that's exactly what I'm going to do. Here are five reasons why you should believe Allah is the Creator of the universe.

1. The first argument is from 'The Divine Reality: God, Islam & The Mirage of Atheism' by Hamza Andreas Tzortzis. It's an excellent book that I would highly recommend reading.

'Imagine you find yourself sitting in the corner of a room. The door that you entered through is now completely sealed, and there is no way of entering or exiting. The walls, ceiling and floor are made up of stone. All you can do is stare into an open, empty space surrounded by cold, dark and stony walls. Due to immense boredom, you fall asleep. A few hours pass by, you wake up. As you open your eyes, you are shocked to see that in the middle of the room is a desk with a computer on top of it. You approach the desk and notice some words on the computer screen: This desk and computer came from nothing.

Do you believe what you have read on the screen? Of course, you do not. At first glance, you rely on your intuition that it is impossible for the computer and the desk to have appeared from no prior activity or cause. Then you start to think about what could possibly have happened. After some thought, you realise a limited number of reasonable explanations. The first is that they could have come from no causal conditions or prior activity—in other words, nothing. The second is that they could have caused or created themselves. The third is that they could have been created or placed there by some prior cause. Since your cognitive faculties are normal and in working order, you conclude that the third explanation is the most rational.

Although this form of reasoning is universal, a more robust variation of the argument can be found eloquently summarised in the Qur'an. The argument states that the possible explanations for a finite entity coming into being could be that it came from nothing, it created itself, it could have been created by something else created, or it was created by something uncreated. Before I break down the argument further, it must be noted that the Qur'an often presents rational, intellectual arguments. The Qur'an is a persuasive and powerful text that seeks to engage its reader. Hence it positively imposes itself on our minds and hearts, and it achieves this by asking profound questions and presenting powerful arguments.

The Qur'anic argument

The Qur'an provides a powerful argument for God's existence: *'Or were they created by nothing? Or were they the creators [of themselves]? Or did they create the heavens and Earth? Rather, they are not certain.' (Surah 52, Verses 35 and 36)*

Although this argument refers to the human being, it can also be applied to anything that began to exist or anything that emerged. The Qur'an uses the word *khuliqu*, which means created, made or originated. So it can refer to anything that came into being. Now let us break down the argument. The Qur'an mentions four possibilities to explain how something was created or came into being or existence:

- Created by nothing: 'or were they created by nothing?'
- Self-created: 'or were they the creators of themselves?'

- Created by something created: 'or did they create the heavens and the Earth?', which implies a created thing being ultimately created by something else created.

- Created by something uncreated: 'Rather, they are not certain', implying that the denial of God is baseless, and therefore the statement implies that there is an uncreated creator.

2. Imam Abu Hanifah's conversation with an atheist

Long ago, in Baghdad, there was a Muslim empire. On one side of the River Tigris were the royal palaces and the city on the other. The Muslims were gathered in the royal court when an atheist approached them. He said to them, 'I don't believe in God, there cannot be a God, you cannot hear or see Him, you're wasting your time! Bring me your best debater, and I will debate this issue with him.'

The best debater at the time was Imam Abu Hanifah. A messenger from amongst the Muslims was sent over the River Tigris to the city, where Abu Hanifah was, to tell him about the atheist awaiting him. On crossing the River Tigris, the messenger conveyed the news to Abu Hanifah, saying, 'Oh Abu Hanifah, an atheist is waiting for you to debate you, please come!' Abu Hanifah told the messenger that he would be on his way.

The messenger went over the River Tigris again and to the palace, where everyone, including the atheist, awaited the arrival of Abu Hanifah. It was sunset, and one hour had passed, but Abu Hanifah still had yet to arrive. Another hour had passed, but still, no sign of him. The Muslims started to become worried about his late arrival. They did not want the atheist to think that they were too scared to debate him, yet they did not want to take up the challenge themselves as Abu Hanifah was the best debater amongst the Muslims. Another hour passed, and suddenly the atheist laughed and said, 'Your best debater is too scared! He knows he's wrong; he is too frightened to come and debate with me. I guarantee he will not turn up today.'

The Muslims increased in apprehension, and eventually, it had passed midnight, and the atheist had a smile on his face. The clock ticked on, and finally, Abu Hanifah arrived. The Muslims inquired about his lateness and remarked, 'Oh, Abu Hanifah, a messenger sent for you hours ago, and you arrive now, explain your lateness to us.'

Abu Hanifah apologised for his lateness and began to explain. 'Once the messenger delivered the news to me, I began to make my way to the River Tigris, and on reaching the river bank, I realised there was no boat to cross the river. It was getting dark, and I looked around; there was no boat anywhere, nor was there a navigator or a sailor for me to cross the river to get to the royal palaces. I continued looking for a boat, as I did not want the atheist to think I was running away and did not want to debate with him.

I was standing on the river bank looking for a navigator or a boat when something caught my attention in the middle of the river. I looked forward, and to my amazement, I saw planks of wood rising to the surface from the sea bed. I was shocked and amazed. I couldn't believe what I was seeing. I continued to look into the middle of the river and saw nails coming up from the sea floor. They positioned themselves onto the boat and held the planks together. I stood in shock and thought to myself, 'Oh Allah, how can this happen, planks of wood rising to the surface by themselves, and then nails positioning themselves onto the boat without

11

being banged?' I could not understand what was happening before my eyes.'

The atheist, meanwhile, was listening with a smile on his face. Abu Hanifah continued, 'I was still standing on the river bank watching these planks of wood join together with nails. I could see water seeping through the gaps in the wood, and unexpectedly I saw a sealant appear from the river, and it began sealing the gaps without someone having poured it. Again I thought, 'Ya Allah, how is this possible? How can sealant appear and seal the gaps without someone having poured it, and nails appear without someone having banged them?' I looked closer and saw a boat forming before my eyes.

Suddenly, a sail appeared, and I thought, 'How is this happening? A boat has appeared before my eyes, planks of wood, nails, sealant and now a sail, but how can I use this boat to cross the river to the royal palaces?' I stood staring in wonderment, and suddenly the boat began to move. It came towards me against the current. It stood floating beside me while I was on the river bank as if telling me to embark on it. I went on the boat, and yet again, it began to move.

There was no navigator or sailor on the boat, and the boat began to travel in the direction of the royal palaces without anyone having programmed it as to where to go. I could not understand what was happening and how this boat had formed and was taking me to my destination against the water flow. The boat eventually reached the other side of the River Tigris, and I disembarked. I turned around, and the boat had disappeared, which is why I am late.'

At this moment, the atheist laughed and remarked, 'Oh, Abu Hanifah, I heard that you were the best debater amongst the Muslims. I heard that you were the wisest, the most knowledgeable among your people. I can say that you show none of these qualities from seeing you today. You speak of a boat appearing from nowhere without someone having built it. Nails positioning themselves without someone having banged them, sealant being poured without someone having poured it, and the boat taking you to your destination without a navigator against the tide, I swear I do not believe a word of it!'

Abu Hanifah turned to the atheist and replied, 'You don't believe a word of it? That nails can appear by themselves? Or sealant can be poured by itself? You don't believe that a boat can move without a navigator; hence you don't believe that a boat can appear without a boat maker?' The atheist said, 'Yes, I don't believe a word of it!'

Abu Hanifah replied, 'If you cannot believe that a boat came into being without a boat maker, then this is only a boat; how can you think that the whole universe, the stars, the oceans, and the planets came into being without a creator? The atheist, astonished at his reply, got up and fled. (Transcribed from a lecture by Ahmad Ali)

3. Nature points to a Creator

The Quran contains numerous verses encouraging us to consider the beauty of the universe surrounding us. All of these things point to a Creator. Like an artist's motif found all over his works. The Creator of all of these is one. The beauty of the planets that swiftly travel in their specific orbits, as well as other celestial bodies; if these were even slightly out of their orbit, it would result in a disaster, the extent of which only Allah knows. Since their inception, they have adhered to a strict system. Allah states: *'He created the sun, the moon, and the stars—all subjected by His command. The creation and the command belong to Him (alone). Blessed is Allah—Lord of all worlds!' (Surah Al-Araf, 7:54)*

Allah advises us to look at our bodies: *'And on the earth are signs for the certain [in faith]. And in your own selves. Then will you not see?' (Surah Adh-Dhariyat, 51:20-21)*

To contemplate the countless animals inhabiting the planet in a diverse range of sizes and characteristics. Allah states: *'Allah has created every [living] creature from water. And of them are those that move on their bellies, and of them are those that walk on two legs, and of them are those that walk on four. Allah creates what He wills. Indeed, Allah is over all things competent.' (Surah An-Noor, 24:45)*

Thinking about these creatures helps to boost your faith in Allah: *'Do you not see that Allah sends down rain from the sky, and We produce thereby fruits of varying colours? And in the mountains are tracts, white and red of varying shades and [some] extremely black. And among people and moving creatures are grazing livestock are various colours similarly. Only those fear Allah, from among His slaves who have knowledge. Indeed, Allah is Exalted in Might and Forgiving.' (Surah Fatir, 35:27-28)*

4. Fixed natural laws govern all living things

The universe operates by uniform laws of nature. Much of life may seem uncertain but look at what we can count on day after day: gravity is always there, keeping us on the ground, a hot cup of tea left on a counter will get cold, the sun rises in the morning and sets in the evening, the speed of light never changes. How is it that we can identify laws of nature that never change? Why is the universe so orderly, so reliable?

Humans need food, water, air, heat and sunlight. We depend on these things but have no control over them. We're not as self-sufficient as we think. Who is ensuring we get these necessities every day? You could say we're a bit like a kitten that depends on its carer for milk. But who is generously taking care of our needs every day?

We share certain instincts with animals; no one tells us we must have family and friends; we just crave company. We cannot survive on our own. Once you reach puberty, you begin to find boys attractive. We have no control over how our bodies change during puberty. Who put those feelings, needs and desires inside us?

Humans are very smart; scientists can clone animals, transplant hearts, fertilise eggs in Petri dishes, and plastic surgeons can restructure your nose and give you a tummy tuck, but they can only work with an existing human body; they can't give life to a dead person or stop a person from dying. The complexity of the laws of nature point to a deliberate designer, Allah, who not only created us with needs but then mercifully sustains and provides for us.

5. You don't have to see Allah to know He exists

Why can't I see my Creator? That's a good question. On the other hand, are there things you believe in but can't see? i.e. gravity, love, jealousy, you can only see their effects or results, but you can't touch or feel them. You can think and reason; the difference between animals and us is that we can understand things even if we can't see them. An animal must see or sense danger, and then it will react. We can understand something is dangerous even if we don't see or experience it, right?

Would we deny the artist existed if we see paintings without seeing the artist in action? In the same way, we believe that Allah created everything without having to see Him (or touch, or hear, etc.). In an ideal world, if we could see Allah, then everyone would believe in Him and obey Him, there would be no atheists, and everyone would be Muslim and live happily ever after in jannah... However, Allah, in His wisdom, has decided that we cannot see Him in this world. When He created us, He gave us the free will and intelligence to either acknowledge the multitudes of signs that point to Him being the designer and Creator of the universe or to deny His presence as a test for humanity.

Wise words from Imam Al-Shafi

The great scholar of Islam, Imam Al-Shafi (d. 820), was asked about the Creator's existence, and he responded, 'The leaves of a berry bush all have one taste. Worms eat it and produce silk. Bees eat it and produce honey. Goats, camels, and cows eat it and deliver offspring. Deer eat it and produce musk. Yet, all of these come from one thing.'

Another eminent scholar Imam Aḥmad (d. 855), was asked about the Creator's existence, and he replied, 'Consider a smooth, impenetrable fortress without any doors or exits. The outside is like white silver, and the inside is like pure gold. It is built in this way, and behold! Its walls crack, and out comes an animal hearing and seeing with a beautiful shape and a pleasant voice.' Imam Aḥmad was referring to the natural wonder of a baby chick emerging from its mother's egg.

The clear evidence in God's signs requires no specialised religious training or knowledge to understand and believe in them. It is natural and intuitive to recognise them. In a well-known story, a Bedouin—a member of the nomad tribes who were usually illiterate—was asked about the Creator's existence and replied, 'Glory be to Allah! The camel's droppings testify to the existence of the camel, and the footprints testify to the existence of the walker. A sky that holds the stars, a land that has fairways, and a sea that has waves? Does not all of this testify to the existence of the Kind, the Knowing?'

To sum up, in the Quran, Allah encourages us to use our minds and realise Allah has created the world around us. When your belief is founded on certainty, you will be confident that the Islamic rules you follow are correct.

'Indeed, in the creation of the heavens and the earth and the alternation of the night and the day are signs for those of understanding.' (Ali-Imran,3:190)

'And Allah has sent down rain from the sky and given life thereby to the earth after its lifelessness. Indeed, in that is a sign for a people who listen.' (An Nahl, 16:65)

'This is the creation of Allah. So, show Me what those other than Him have created. Rather, the wrongdoers are in clear error.' (Surah Luqman, 31: 11)

WHY THE QURAN IS THE WORD OF ALLAH

Once you're sure Allah is your Creator; how do you know how to worship Him? Why did Allah create you, and how will you find out? Some people believe they can decide on their own how they will worship their Creator. They want to choose their spiritual path. They see belief as a personal spiritual journey; everyone should be free to 'find God or a Goddess' in their own way and do what makes them spiritually happy.

Strange spirituality

Personalised spirituality and making up your own religious rules are problematic. What if your spiritual practices cause harm to others? For example, the Aztecs worshipped many gods; the most important was their sun god, Huitzilopochtli; they believed that their 'good' gods should be kept strong to keep away the 'bad' gods by making human sacrifices.

The ancient Egyptians also sacrificed people as part of their Pharaoh's burial rites. The Pharaoh's servants would be killed after the Pharaoh died so, supposedly, they could accompany him to the afterlife. They believed that what belonged to the Pharaoh on Earth also belonged to him in the next life, and he should be able to enjoy his possessions in the afterlife. These two historical examples show that when people decide how to worship their Creator, it can lead to irrational and gruesome rituals.

Spiritual Gurus

Strange things are happening in the West; a growing number of non-Muslims are rejecting God. So, where do they look for guidance instead? Atheist spiritual gurus. Have you heard the expression, 'The universe is sending me a message?' It's all over Instagram. It's trendy to 'believe in the power of the universe.' Take note of how they refer to the universe as if it were God. Manifestation gurus like Rhonda Byrne, author of The Secret and Sarah Prout are making millions preaching to women to manifest their desires.

'You have the power to create your own reality and manifest your dreams when you connect to the energy of the universe. Now you can easily and effortlessly call upon the universe for the wisdom, guidance and clarity you need to manifest your goals, dreams, wishes and desires... *faster than ever before.*' Sarah Prout[2]

The basic assumption is foolish and intellectually dishonest - I'm referring to the trending idea of praying to the universe. Prout prays to 'dear universe' for help and signs. As if a galaxy cluster has the power to hear and comfort her. Planets don't have the power to change their own orbit; how are they going to change another creation's destiny?

I suppose that in the Atheist culture, people desperately seek something to pray to, and the universe serves as a substitute for God. They believe that because the universe is personal, with human feelings and its own will, it will bestow personal favours on them. In effect, they flee from one extreme (the absence of God) to another (everything is God). Spiritual gurus are con artists taking advantage of confused people desperate for spiritual guidance. This is spiritual commodification.

Witchy spiritualism is trendy

Did you know that across America, the practice of witchcraft and paganism is growing among young women? It's bizarre! Witches have long been a part of pop culture, but for all the attention paid to them, few people realise a subculture of young women practice paganism because they think it'll make their lives better.

In an interview for Teen Vogue, Moon Church member Molly explains the allure of witchcraft 'My best friend and I were always fascinated with matters of the occult,' says college freshman Emma, who started a coven three years ago in her hometown in Oregon. 'We loved *The Craft*, and the Ouija board came out at every sleepover. That was how we bonded. In high school, we started studying Wicca together, looking up stuff online and learning how to do rituals and spells. A couple of our friends would join us for gatherings, and it became like a sisterhood to me.'[3]

Why witchcraft?

One reason naive young women embrace witchcraft is that there is an immense spiritual void in western societies. Christianity no longer makes sense and is riddled with contradictions. Whereas being a witch allows you to pick and mix your spirituality with no hard and fast rules. You can make up your beliefs and do whatever you want: cast an obsession spell on your crush, invoke a curse on everyone you hate; the nonsensical list is never ending...

Like many of her sisters in Moon Church, Molly adheres to a collection of beliefs rooted in pagan rituals, Eastern traditions of meditation and yoga, magic, and even artistic processes like writing and performing. The key here is individualism. Few witches follow ancient pagan traditions to an exact degree, instead developing a personal system that draws upon multiple sources.[4]

The embrace of all things witchy makes perfect sense at a moment when teenage girls are more self-possessed than ever. 'Today's young women are taught to value power, beauty, and sexuality, but on their own terms,' says Pam Grossman, author of *What Is a Witch*. And even better, as Grossman tells it you don't need a membership card to be a part of the coven. 'Witchcraft is about magic, and at its core, that's about manifest-ing what you want,' she says. 'Conjuring your life on your own terms.' With so many social issues swirling on top of our personal daily dramas, magic offers a sense of control in the chaos. Consider it a way to channel all of the latent energy — anger, confusion, or grief — into good.'[5]

Teenage witches cause confusion

Being a witch sounds so positive 'Forge your own path to the divine, all you need is the desire to do so. Candles and incense and beautiful sur-roundings sure help, but magic comes from within.'[6] But the bottom line is believing witchcraft is real makes as much sense as believing in unicorns: it's fantasy. How can you take anything TikTok witches says seriously when they admit they learnt their manifestations from the TV series Sabrina The Teenage Witch and the movie Hocus Pocus? Long story short, they are unhappy teenagers desperate for hope and community but also delusional: they think they are new-age messengers!

'After going through a dark time and starting my healing journey, I rapidly went to different awakenings and gained lots of spiritual knowledge. So, I started sharing that with TikTok, and as my community grew, I realised helping others with their own spirituality and healing is something I'm meant to do.'7

Modern day witches have no spiritual knowledge and are misleading young women, telling them it's okay to believe what you want. There is no tangible evidence or truth behind tarot cards, moon water, manifestations and menstrual cycle rituals. Human beings cannot determine for themselves how to worship their Creator; rather, the Creator has to inform us how this is done. This is through messengers and revealed books.

So how can we communicate with our Creator?
We can't directly talk to Allah, so it makes sense that Allah will communicate with us to answer all the questions we naturally have about our purpose in life. Throughout time and even today, some people claim they are messengers of Allah.

If someone came to you today and said, 'I am a messenger from Allah, I will tell you how He wants you to live your life; you should follow me', what would you say to them? Of course, you would be sceptical and ask for proof—a sign, something miraculous that could only be from Allah.

A miracle is something which surpasses human capacity. A magic trick or lucky charm won't suffice. As we know, there are con artists who pretend they can communicate with Allah and charge people to pray for them. These self-styled saints prey on desperate people trying to connect with Allah. In the Quran, we are told about genuine messengers, and Allah gave them miraculous signs to prove they are not fake. Let's take a look at the examples of Prophet Sulaiman (as) and Prophet Musa (as).

Prophet Sulaiman (as)

Allah gave him many unique abilities. He was granted the power to understand the speech of birds and animals and control the wind and Jinn. *'So, We subjected to him the wind blowing by his command, gently, wherever he directed' (Surah Sad,38:36).*

'[Sulaiman said] O people, we have been taught the language of birds...' (An-Naml, 27:16).

'And gathered for Sulaiman were his soldiers of the Jinn and men and birds' (An- Naml, 27: 17).

'Indeed, the example of Jesus to Allah is like that of Adam. He created Him from dust; then He said to him, 'Be,' and he was' (Surah Ali Imran 3:59). What is impressive is that Isa (as) is mentioned 25 times throughout the Qur'an, and Adam (as) is also mentioned 25 times! This symmetry could not have been a coincidence.

Quran Facts

Here are some essential facts you should know about the Quran. The Quran was revealed over 23 years. A complete surah (chapter) would not always be revealed all in one go; they were revealed partially, a few ayahs at a time. During the Prophet's (saw) lifetime, the Quran did not exist in book form as we know it today. There were no ayah numbers or surah numbers; this came later. Each year during Ramadan, the Prophet (saw) would recite all the Quran revealed so far with Angel Jibrael. Jibrael then told Prophet Muhammad (saw) the place and order of each ayah. This was all done orally. The Prophet (saw) would memorise an ayah and teach it to the Muslims, who would, in turn memorise it.

Also, the Quran is not organised in chronological order, i.e., Surah Alaq, 96 is not the first surah of the Quran, even though the first ayat to be revealed were from this surah. Having understood the above facts, let's look at the longest surah in the Quran, Surah Al Baqarah; it has 286 ayat. This surah was revealed in stages over almost ten years. In ayah 143 of Surah Al Baqarah Allah says, *'And like that, we made you all a middle nation...'.*

The word 'wasat' means middle and is only used once in the Quran. Miraculously this word middle (wasat) comes in the middle ayah of this surah, there is no way Muhammad (saw) could have organised this ayah to be precisely in the middle of this surah, as he didn't have the Quran in written form, and he couldn't read or write Arabic.

The challenge in the Quran

In the Quran, Allah directly challenged the Arabs to produce a literary work similar to the Quran. Still, they were unable to do so despite their well-known Arabic eloquence. At that time, composing poetry was one of the most admired skills in society, and Arab poets excelled in their use of the Arabic language. The challenge to reproduce the Quran was presented to the Arabs and humanity in three stages: In the Quran, Allah says,

'Say: 'If all mankind and the jinn would come together to produce the like of this Quran, they could not produce it's like even though they exerted all and their strength in aiding one another.' (Al-Isra,17:88).

Next, Allah made the challenge easier,

'Or do they say that he has invented it? Say (to them), 'Bring ten invented chapters like it, and call (for help) on whomever you can besides God if you are truthful.' (Hud,11:13).

This last challenge was to produce a single chapter,

'And if you all are in doubt about what I have revealed to My servant, bring a single chapter like it, and call your witnesses besides God if you are truthful.' (Al Baqarah, 2:23).

These challenges were not just empty words with no one trying to prove them wrong. Prophet Muhammad's (saw) call to end idolatry threatened the oppressive system of Meccan society and the authoritarian position of the ruling Quraishi tribe, who desperately wanted to stop the spread of Islam. Yet, all the Prophet's (saw) opponents had to do to extinguish Islam was to produce a single chapter like any of those the Prophet (saw) and his followers were reciting to the people. Would this have been so difficult for them? Wasn't the Quran in their native language, and weren't they masters of that same language?

Given that the shortest surah in the Quran is Al-Kauthar, which is three ayahs long, essentially, they only had to produce three ayahs like it. Despite this, several Quraishi poets tried to imitate the Quran but failed dismally. In addition, Allah informs us that he will protect the Quran. In Surah Al-Hijr, 15:9, Allah says,

'Indeed, it is We who sent down the Qur'an, and indeed, We will be its guardian.' So, we can confidently say that the Quran we have today is precisely the same as the one revealed to the Prophet Muhammad (saw); nothing has changed.

The Quran is not the speech of Muhammad (saw)

It is well known that Muhammad (saw) could not read or write Arabic. When an ayah was revealed, the Prophet (saw) would recite it to his companions, and they would memorise it. He would not edit the content or change it. In Mecca, Muhammad (saw) faced a lot of hostility from the leaders of Quraish: they would do anything to stop people from embracing Islam. Nevertheless, they never alleged that the Quran was Muhammad's (saw) speech: they knew it was absurd. How could he (saw) write a verses he couldn't read?

How Muhammad (saw) spoke was very different from how the Quran is written. We know how Muhammad (saw) spoke because we have hundreds of his authentic sayings – hadith. Hadith were very carefully collected and saved and put into books. If you were to compare any of these hadith to any verse of the Quran, there would be no similarity between them in style.

The only thing that they claimed was that Muhammad (saw) had got the Quran from a Christian youth called Jabr. Allah refuted this accusation in the Quran and said: *'We know indeed that they say it is a man that taught him. The tongue of him they wickedly point to is notably foreign, while this is Arabic, pure and clear.' (An Nahl, 16:103)*

Historical Miracles

'Pharaoh said, 'Haman, build me a tall tower so I may reach the ropes that lead to the heavens to look for this God of Moses.'

(Surah Ghafir, 40:36-37).

Egyptology is the study of ancient Egyptian history, language, hiero-glyphics, religion, architecture and art. In the late 1800, hieroglyphics were revived by German and French scholars. They travelled to Egypt, studied hieroglyphics, developed a scheme of spellings for the images and turned them into pronounceable words. They began translating the hieroglyphics into documents and learnt a lot about Egyptian court life, the life of the pharaohs, their names and minister's names, and their roles. One of the Pharaoh's ministers in charge of stone quarries and construc-tion was called none other than...Haman!

Haman was mentioned in the Quran. It would have been impossible for anyone living in Arabia in the 7th century to have known his name, as hieroglyphics were no longer used since the 5th century. So, the name was discovered in the 1900s; no one knew his name, but Allah knew this man's name and had revealed it in the Quran.

Scientific facts in the Quran

In the following verse, Allah revealed to the Prophet (saw), 1,500 years ago, the different stages of pregnancy. Ayat, like these, are signs or proofs for all rational people that the Quran is the speech of our Creator, as there is no way any person could have known this information 1500 years ago in the deserts of Arabia.

'Then We made the sperm-drop into a clinging clot, and We made the clot into a lump [of flesh], and We made [from] the lump, bones, and We cov-

ered the bones with flesh; then We developed him into another creation. So, blessed is Allah, the best of creators.' (Al- Muminun, 23:14)

Water is the basis of all life in surah An-Noor Allah informs us,

'Allah created every creature from water. Among them are some that crawl on their bellies, some that walk on two legs and others that walk on all four. Allah creates whatever He wants, for Allah has power over all things.' (An-Noor, 24:45)

So, having looked at all these examples, we can undoubtedly say that the Quran is the speech of Allah, and it is a miracle. Since Muhammad (saw) is the one who brought the Quran, he is a Messenger of Allah. Allah commands us to obey Him and His Messenger and warns us against defying him and imitating the disbelievers who reject him. *'O believers! Obey Allah and His Messenger, and do not turn away from him while you hear. Do not be like those who say, 'We hear,' but in fact; they are not listening.' (Al-Anfal, 20-21)*

Allah chose Prophet Muhammad (saw) to deliver His final message to us via the Quran, and in its pages, we can find the answers to all the crucial questions we have, such as: What is the meaning of life? Why did Allah create me? What happens after I die? How can I achieve peace of mind and happiness in my life? How can I deal with the daily challenges I face? By following in the footsteps of the Prophet (saw), you will not only be proving your love for the messenger (saw), but you will also attain the love of Allah, as mentioned in the Quran. *'Say, (O Muhammad),*

'If you should love Allah, then follow me, (so) Allah will love you and forgive you your sins. And Allah is Forgiving and Merciful.' (Ali-Imran, 3:31)

Quran studies

The Quran is your book of guidance and a way to achieve spiritual progress. It outlines values and beliefs that can make you the best person you can be. It teaches a way of thinking that is positive and enlightened. I would highly recommend enrolling in a regular Quran, hadith and seerah studies classes to understand the meaning of the Quran. You will have many questions, so you need trustworthy teachers to help you. Social media has its place but can never replace studying with qualified teachers. You wouldn't dream of doing your GCSE or A-level exams with social media as your teacher; the same level of study has to be given to Islam. Alhamdullilah, there are many in-person and online Islamic studies classes, I'm sure with the help of your family, you will find something that will suit your needs. Inshallah, as a young, intelligent Muslimah, now is the perfect time to begin your journey as a student of knowledge.

Ibn Abbas reported: The Messenger of Allah (saw) said, *'Take advantage of five before five: your youth before your old age, your health before your illness, your riches before your poverty, your free time before your work, and your life before your death.' Source: Shu'ab al-Imān 9767.*

WHAT IS YOUR PURPOSE IN LIFE?

This is not a question you're asked very often. In contrast, you are constantly asked to think about what you want to study at college or university. What job do you want? What are your career goals? These are all important questions, you should research your options carefully and ask people with wisdom and experience, such as parents, older siblings, career advisors and extended family.

Having said that, I believe society makes us focus too much on study, work, and career and doesn't encourage us to think about the bigger picture. As if they are the most important aspects of life. By the way, I'm not saying you shouldn't study or work. So, what do I mean? You can be a Nobel Prize winner or a CEO of an FTSE100 company, but if you don't have clear answers to the following questions, then your life will lack meaning, and all the money in the world will not make you content. Here are the questions:

- Where did I come from?
- What is my purpose in life?

Let's explore the answers to these questions, knowing that only Allah can give us the answers. Allah created us; it was not down to chance or evolution. He then sent us guidance via the Quran and Sunnah to teach us how to live a balanced, purposeful life. And we are told we will return to Him, and our deeds will be judged.

'Blessed is the One in Whose Hands rests all authority. And He is Most Capable of everything. He is the One` Who created death and life in order to test which of you is best in deeds. And He is the Almighty, All-Forgiving.' (Al-Mulk, 67:1)

When you speak to Muslim converts, they are so happy to receive the certainty of Allah's guidance. Sylvie Fawzy, a French lady who became Muslim, said: 'In Islam, I found a way of life that answers all questions and organises man's life in a way that benefits him and is suited to his nature, with regard to his clothing, his food, his work, his marriage, his choices in life, and his relationship with others.' So it comes as no surprise that the one who adheres to Islam feels content and secure, which are the most important factors in life.[8]

For many of us, just living a happy life would be nice. Interestingly, there is no single definition of happiness; it is subjective to the person experiencing it because it is based on how you feel about your life, i.e. how content you are. How optimistic you are about your future. What techniques you have for dealing with the difficulties you will inevitably face.

Happiness in Islam

To truly be happy, you must first understand your life's purpose. Why did Allah create you? This may be a subject that you are already clear about. If you are certain about life's fundamental questions, then that's brilliant! However, it's perfectly normal for you to have questions about Islam. You may not have had an opportunity to learn about your faith, or you may have adopted it without thinking - and it's crucial to find answers to your questions. Allah says in the Quran that we should use our intellect. That's what differentiates us from animals:

'Indeed, in the creation of the heavens and the earth and the alternation of the night and the day are signs for those of understanding.' (Ali-Imran, 3:190)

So, why did Allah create us?

He created us (humankind) to serve Him. In the Quran, Allah says:

'I have not created men except that they should worship Me.' (Adh-Dhariyat, 51:56)

Worship in Islam is not what most people think it is. It's important to know that Islam is not a religion like Christianity or Hinduism. Religions like these focus on how a person can individually and collectively pray to God, a moral code, and rituals relating to birth, marriage, and death. Their religious texts do not have comprehensive rules about gender relations, inheritance, or how to make treaties between governments.

In contrast, Islam is a holistic way of life. We have detailed laws relating to personal and collective religious rituals, social matters, education, morals, economics, politics and international relations. It extends over the entire spectrum of life, showing us how to conduct all human activities in a just manner. Worship can be seen in every act we perform. How we communicate with others, and the acts of compassion we perform daily. When you focus on pleasing Allah, your actions become an act of worship.

Worship is a broad concept in Islam. It refers to loving Allah, pleasing Him, knowing Him, and dedicating all acts of worship to Him alone, such as prayer and supplication. Worshipping Allah is the ultimate goal of our existence; it liberates us from slavery to our desires, other people and social expectations.

'Did you think that We had created you in play (without any purpose) and that you would not be brought back to Us?' (Al-Mumenoon, 23:115)

Regarding the creation of the world, Allah says:

'And to Allah belongs the dominion of the heavens and the earth, and Allah is over all things competent. Indeed, the creation of the heavens and the earth and the alternation of the night and the day are signs for those of understanding. Who remember Allah while standing or sitting or [lying] on their sides and give thought to the creation of the heavens and the earth, [saying], 'Our Lord, You did not create this aimlessly; exalted are You [above such a thing]; then protect us from the punishment of the Fire...' (Ali' Imran, 3: 189-191)

In the Qur'an, Allah presents us with a thought-provoking example: *'God puts forward this illustration: can a man who has for his masters several partners at odds with each other be considered equal to a man devoted wholly to one master? All praise belongs to God, though most of them do not know.' (Az-Zumar, 39: 29)*

Today, in a whirlwind of distractions it's too easy to follow other than Allah and his Messenger (saw). Many ideas exist in broader society that are at odds with Islam and are competing for your attention. Teenagers have many 'masters' who do not have their best interests at heart. Think about it. Who has the most influence over your actions? Your friends, TikTokers, Youtubers, Netflix or Allah and His Messenger (saw)? Whose content are you consuming the most? What are you devoting your time and energy to? Since at least 2019, Facebook employees have been researching the effect of Instagram on the mental health of its younger users. Their research has repeatedly found that it harms a large percentage of the population, especially teenage girls.

'We make body image issues worse for one in three teen girls,' said a slide from one internal presentation in 2019. Another transatlantic study found more than 40% of Instagram users who reported feeling 'unattractive' said the feeling began on the app; about a quarter of the teenagers who reported feeling 'not good enough' said it started on Instagram.[9]

Being constantly bombarded with photos of the 'perfect' life and seemingly ideal bodies can negatively impact how you feel about your life and looks. It can be tough not to compare yourself to others, but please remember all the holiday pics and outfits people post are filtered and enhanced. A spokesperson for the 5Rights Foundation sums up the intentions of social media companies. 5Rights Foundation works for reforms to digital services to make them more appropriate for children and young people:

'In pursuit of profit, these companies are stealing children's time, self-esteem and mental health, and sometimes tragically their lives … This is an entirely human-made world, largely privately owned, designed to optimise for commercial purposes.'[10]

The multi-million dollar cosmetic industry slyly makes you feel ugly. Their marketing strategy is simple: make you unhappy with your skin, eyelashes, pigmentation, eyebrows etc. Once you feel ugly and are vulnerable, they persuade you to buy an endless supply of flawless concealers, highlighters, and false eyelashes to 'solve your beauty dilemmas.'

Here's a typical advert, notice how they make you feel you are doing yourself a favour by buying their products: 'Take your lashes to the next level with volume that doesn't quit. For the long, glamorous lash look you can't get enough of, you need our go-big-or-go-home Volum' Express mascara. Isn't it time you had show-stopping eyes? To find the formula made with you in mind, scroll on...'[11]

An environmentally unfriendly fashion industry grooms you to be obsessed with your appearance: a hyper-consumer who buys clothes even though she doesn't need them: 'Stay ahead of the game with our 'New in' edit, featuring new women's clothing and the latest fashion trends. From belts to bags and caps to cover-ups, find that finishing touch under all your fave brands. ASOS DESIGN serves bits that are always ready for the gram, whether it's super-chunky sandals or a lovely lil dress – start scrolling for some serious inspo. And if you're in the running to become CEO of trends, remember to bookmark this tab, cos the latest fashion changes all the time.'[12]

For teenagers, the entertainment industry predominantly creates shows like Euphoria, which normalises risky sexual behaviour, experimentation with drugs and alcohol, and LGBTQI+ as applaudable lifestyles. I'm sure you are wondering why these industries believe they can insult your intelligence. The life goals they want you to pursue will not give you peace of mind or success in this life or the next. Unfortunately, depression and eating disorders have become increasingly common among American teenagers – especially teen girls, who are now almost three times as likely as teen boys to have had recent experiences with depression. [13]

In contrast, Allah understands you better than you know yourselves. He has more mercy for you than your parents, and He informs you that He is your true master and that you can only be content by worshipping Him alone. In her book, Reclaim Your Heart, Yasmin Mogahed eloquently describes the emptiness we feel when the light of Islam does not guide our lives.

'Every time you run after, seek, or petition something weak or feeble… you, too, become weak or feeble. Even if you do reach that which you seek, it will never be enough. You will soon need to seek something else. You will never reach true contentment or satisfaction. That is why we live in a world of trade-ins and upgrades. Your phone, your car, your computer, your woman, your man can always be traded in for a newer, better model. However, there is a freedom from that slavery. When the object upon which you place all your weight is unshaking, unbreakable, and unending, you cannot fall.'[14]

Society tells you that if you are rich, you'll be happy; you have made it as a young woman if you are fair-skinned, tall, and skinny if you have thousands of Instagram followers and a popular TikTok account. They are the things that will bring you endless joy. To want money and nice things isn't wrong. Just don't allow your looks, making money and buying stuff to define who you are; having these things alone will not bring you happiness and contentment. The experiences of two famous Indian Muslim actresses, Sana Khan and Zaira Wasim, starkly illustrate this.

In October 2020, the Bollywood actress Sana Khan decided to leave the film industry; she wrote a detailed post on Instagram explaining her reasons:

'Brothers and sisters … Today I am talking to you at an important point in my life. I have been living the life of show biz for years, and during this time, I got all kinds of fame, respect and wealth from my loved ones. For which I am thankful to them.

But, for the last few days, a thought has kept me occupied. I have been wondering, does one take birth only to earn wealth and fame for oneself? Isn't it a moral responsibility of humans to serve or support those who are helpless or needy? Shouldn't people think about what will happen to them in the afterlife since one can die at any given time?

I have been finding answers to these questions for a very long time, especially the second question about what will happen to me in my afterlife. When I looked for answers to these questions in my religion, I found out that we take birth in this worldly life to make our afterlife better in many ways. And it will only be better when one leads his/her life according to the commandments of his/her Creator and does not make money and fame their only objective in life. Instead, one should stay away from the world of sin and serve humanity, walking in the direction and path laid down by his/her Creator. This is the reason why today I declare that I have resolved to renounce this showbiz (film industry) and wish to serve humanity and follow the orders of my Creator.

All brothers and sisters are requested to pray for me to Allah to accept my repentance and grant me the true ability to live in accordance with my determination to spend my life following the commandments of my Creator and in the service of humanity and grant me perseverance. Finally, all brothers and sisters are requested to not contact me with regards to any showbiz-related work or invite me for any industry-related events henceforth,' Sana concluded.

Sana is not the first Muslim actress who has left the film industry to serve 'Islam' and follow Allah's 'modest' rules. A few years ago, 'Dangal' and 'Secret Superstar' actress Zaira Wasim announced her retirement from acting in an Instagram letter. 'Bollywood took me away from Islam,' she writes in the six-page letter, citing interference with her religious practices as the reason for her decision.

Despite her fame and success, she stated that she was not truly satisfied with her line of work. She was asked to star in a movie with Shah Rukh Khan which would have made her an A-list celebrity but she chose Islam instead. It was when she tried adjusting to her new lifestyle that she re-alised her job had influenced her relationship with Allah. When talking about her difficulties, Zaira Wasim says 'she has found solace in Allah and the Quran.'

Both actresses returned to their 'original state' which is what Islam calls 'fitra'. Fitra is an inbuilt instinct we all have, given by our Creator, to gravitate towards Allah. The further we are from Allah, the more our minds and emotional state remain uneasy.

Sayyiduna Abu Hurayrah narrated the Prophet (saw) informed us that *'Every child is born on 'fitrah' (the natural inclination to Islam); however-er, the child's parents make him a Jew or Christian. It is as an animal delivers a perfect baby animal. Do you find it mutilated?' (Muslim)*

This hadith does not literally mean that everyone is born with faith, that is, with a belief in Allah and his Messengers. Rather that everyone is born in a state where they are pre-programmed to want to believe in Al-lah and to worship and obey Him. This is the innate recognition of Allah that pushes human beings to study deeply with the intellect Allah has given them and conclude that Allah is the one worthy to be worshipped.

What is the secret to a happy life?

Becoming rich, famous and flawless isn't your life's purpose; rather, it is to worship Allah, which leads to happiness even if your life isn't Instagrammable. When we put Allah at the centre of our lives, that's when we will be truly happy and content.

So, what does that mean? How do we do that in our daily lives? It doesn't mean that we have to pray all day and fast and not want anything that gives us pleasure, as the following hadith illustrates:

Anas bin Malik narrated a group of three men came to the houses of the wives of the Prophet (saw) asking how the Prophet (saw) worshipped (Allah). When they were informed about that, they considered their worship insufficient and said, 'Where are we from the Prophet (saw) as his past and future sins have been forgiven.'

Then one of them said, 'I will offer the prayer throughout the night forever.' The other said, 'I will fast throughout the year and will not break my fast.' The third said, 'I will keep away from the women and will not marry forever.' Allah's Messenger (saw) came to them and said, 'Are you the same people who said so-and-so? By Allah, I am more submissive to Allah and more afraid of Him than you; yet I fast and break my fast, I do sleep, and I also marry women. So he who does not follow my tradition in religion is not from me (not one of my followers). (Sahih al-Bukhari)

To lead an Allah-focused life, you need to look at your daily actions and see whether they align with Quran and Sunnah. Before you decide to do something, you need to ask yourself, is this what Allah wants me to do? And have I gained knowledge to find out how Allah instructs me to do it? Are my actions in sync with the Sunnah of the Prophet (saw)? Or am I just doing what will benefit me and make me temporarily happy in this life?

This may seem overwhelming; however, you first need to adopt this mindset and start with baby steps. Many aspects of your life are already in line with Islam. For example, you always check if the food you eat is halal. It would be best if you did the same for the other areas of your life. I.e. how you treat your parents and siblings, the people you choose to be friends with, what clothes you wear, the accounts you follow on TikTok etc.

This is what it means to have taqwa when you are conscious of Allah as you make life choices. We don't just do what makes us happy in the moment; that's what non-Muslims do. That's the difference between us and someone who does not submit to the will of Allah. I'm not telling you to try and overhaul your whole life overnight. Instead, reflect on the different aspects of your life and check whether they align with our sacred text. This will involve gaining knowledge, and that is a good thing. We spend so much time studying for our GCSEs and A-levels we should spend an equal amount of time studying our deen.

A perfect place to start is your salah. Understanding the meaning of the surahs you recite by reading the translation and tafsir. If you are praying your salah regularly, obeying Allah in other areas will soon become more manageable. Inshallah, do lots of dua to Allah to guide you. A very easy way to begin learning about the life of the Prophet (saw) is to read a book of Seerah, the life of the Prophet (saw). The more you know about his (saw) life, the more you will love him and want to follow him.

The Prophet said, 'Verily, my prayer, my rites, my life, and my death are for Allah the Lord of the worlds. He has no partner, and with this, I have been commanded, and I am among the Muslims. O Allah, guide me to the best deeds and the best character, for no one guides to the best of them but you. Protect me from evil deeds and evil character, for no one protects from the evil of them but you.' (Sunan al-Nasā'ī 896)

As Muslims, we recognise that the purpose of our lives is more than to eat, drink, watch Netflix and repeat. Our ultimate goal is to reach jannah. Entertaining ourselves might bring us short-term happiness, but it won't get us closer to jannah. The Messenger of Allah (saw) said,

'The world is a prison for the believer and a paradise for the unbeliever.' (Muslim).

So, the path to true happiness is to seek Allah's pleasure by worshipping Him alone. In the Quran, Allah tells us: *'The believers, men, and women, are Auliyâ' of one another; they enjoin Al-Ma'rûf (good) and forbid from Al-Munkar (evil); they perform As-Salât, and give the Zakât, and obey Allāh and His Messenger. Allāh will have His Mercy on them. Indeed Allāh is All-Mighty, All-Wise. Allāh has promised the believers -men and women – Gardens under which rivers flow to dwell therein forever and beautiful mansions in Gardens of Paradise. But the greatest bliss is the Good Pleasure of Allāh. That is the supreme success.' (At-Tawbah, 9:71-72)*

THE MEANING OF LIFE
Zaynab Mufti

Ask me what life means, I'll tell you I don't know
I'll tell you I've searched, but all I see is the glam and the glow
The go to school, the work, and grow old
Pretend to be happy with what I'm told
Get a 9-5 and make money till I fit the mould

Live life and do what feels nice
Chase pleasure and let my soul pay the price
Look for love and search for my worth
Try and find my purpose on this big, big earth
Or better yet, distract myself so not knowing doesn't hurt

Ask me what life means, I'll tell you I'm still questioning
I'm looking for answers, but my distractions are deafening
I'm searching for peace, but where the world takes me is unsettling

If my life is: eat, sleep, repeat, will this be my condition till I die?
Will I be people-pleasing, ignoring that cry?
The one deep in my soul calling for purpose in my life
Will I survive on getting high and ignoring my inner eye?
The one that can see that there must be more to life
The one that is searching for something to hold on to before I die

Ask me what life means, I'll tell you I'm getting closer

I'm thinking, I'm observing, and I'm starting over
I'm told my purpose is finding success, but by whose measure?
Is success the money, the fame, or giving in to pleasure?
Is success losing control in all of the temporary leisure?
Is it gratification of the self or being a slave to the media?
Is it feeding the ego, letting myself get greedier?
Is my purpose determined by me?
Do I let my friends dictate what I should be?
Is all that exists only the things that I can see?
Is there nothing more that will set me free?

And like Ibrahim, I look to the sky
I come to realise that there's more than meets the eye
If I turn to my surroundings and explore the signs
If I accept that I've been placed in a world that is precise and designed
With every particle intentionally positioned and each aspect of nature
aligned

If I look to the inner workings of the human mind
To the capabilities that I hold and the greatness of humankind
The intricacy of my ears and how my fingerprints have been refined
The positioning of my eyes and the way my stomach has been lined
The pumping of my heart and how my nails are outlined
The veins running through my body distinct and defined
If I see that I had no part in my making, then I think that I will find
Surely, I exist with greater purpose; I am a creation of something divine!

So, I read, and I search, and I reflect
And I plead to know what life means and how to connect

How to discover the purpose that I frantically seek
How to make something of myself so that I am no longer weak
How to bring strength to a life determined by desire
I question, and I ponder, and I conclude that there must be a purpose higher

Ask me what life means, I'll tell you I'm walking towards the light
I'm seeing answers in the changing of the day and in the night
In the rain that falls and the birds that are held up in flight
In the ships that stay afloat and the vastness of the skies
In the mountain tops and the way that they rise
In the winds that blow and the sustenance that grows
In the existence of the fly and the river that flows
In the honey that is produced and the camel that stores fat
In the plants that spring up after winter rendered them flat
In the world around me that puts my mind at rest
That shows me the answer and lightens the weight on my chest
That points to the Maker upon whom I rely
The Being that gave me life and will raise me after He causes me to die
The one who is alone, the Mighty and most High
The Lord of the worlds who has questioned which of His favours I will deny

Ask me what life means, I'll tell you to look
To see for yourself and to read The Book
The guidance that is the answer for all who seek
Sent from above and to you, He speaks
The criterion that is divine and determines my way
That gives me purpose and an order to my day

That urges me to submit, and to Him, I pray

Ask me what life means, I'll tell you to kneel

Head on the ground till you see yourself heal

Filled with purpose and His pleasure you'll feel

Ask me what life means, I'll tell you to worship

To enjoy His bounties and see that it's worth it

To follow His path and to live with intention

For every breath to grant you spiritual ascension

To have reason in every word that you mention

To have purpose in your walk, conscious of His gaze

To plan for the meeting where you'll account for these days

Ask me what life means, I'll tell you I've seen

I've felt the love that to give He is keen

I'll tell you to accept His will and the way of the beloved that He sent

The praised one who you'll follow and then find yourself content

To let go of the pride and do what you can

To honour His creation and be like the man

Who fulfilled the meaning of life and submitted to the King

Who found closeness to Him and showed us that in His praises, we shall

fly, and we shall sing.

DOES ISLAM HAVE TOO MANY RULES?

H ave you heard Muslims say, 'Islam is so strict,' or 'Why can't I just do what my friends are doing?' Maybe you agree with these statements. Let's examine why some may consider following Islamic rules a burden. Where does this idea come from? To begin, I would like you to consider the following questions:

- Do you go to school or college?
- Do you line up in the canteen for lunch?
- Do you adhere to dress codes? i.e. school uniforms or socially accepted clothes in your daily life.
- Do you stop at a crossing when the traffic lights turn green?

These are all actions you carry out. Do you believe they are restrictive? Do you think they're a pain, but you still comply with them because you want to get ahead and succeed in life and avoid getting into trouble?

- Imagine a school without rules: learning would not happen.
- Imagine a country without laws: chaos would ensue, and criminals would go unpunished.
- Imagine a family without rules: individualism and disrespect would prevail. Kids would never get off their phones.

If you think about it, your whole life is governed by rules and laws, for example:

- School rules include exam rules, coursework deadlines, and school holiday dates.

- Workplace rules: answering to a boss, work dress code, work schedule.

Do you have a choice when it comes to obeying rules?

We all have the option of obeying rules or not. We do have a choice. But there are also consequences and punishments for breaking the rules in society. Every nation has laws and regulations to organise society. If you break the rules, you will be considered a criminal and face penalties or do jail time. So our choices are always limited.

When you consider the rules imposed on you by your local council and government, you think they are necessary and helpful in ensuring everything runs smoothly and safely. But, why do you believe that the rules you must follow in Islam are strict, whereas the rules you accept in your social life or school are not restrictive? Do you feel the rules your parents set about going out late, sleepovers, and phones are unfair?

How much freedom do we have?

There is a widespread belief that Western societies are superior because they provide greater personal freedom. People have the freedom to dress however they want, to say whatever they want, and to do whatever they want. But there are limits; they do not have unrestricted freedom. In truth, they have a wide range of options regarding clothing, food, entertainment, relationships, jobs, etc. But no one can deny that they must all abide by the rules and laws of the land. Choice has its limits.

These rules and laws are made by flawed humans, men and women like you and me, who are easily swayed by biases, self-interest and prejudices. Historically, we can see how people's perceptions of what constitutes a good law and what constitutes a bad law shift over time. For example:

- The UK has a long history of racism. Racial discrimination in all aspects of life was commonplace for ethnic minorities in the UK Commonwealth citizens (Jamaicans, Pakistanis, Indians etc.) who were invited to contribute to the 'mother country' after WWII's end were frequently met with 'No Blacks' signs as they looked for housing and jobs. Only in 1965, in the face of fierce Conservative opposition, was a limited piece of legislation, the Race Relations Act passed. It made it illegal to refuse anyone access to public places such as hotels, restaurants, pubs, cinemas, or public transportation based on race. Refusing to rent to people because of their race was also prohibited, and inciting racial hatred -'incitement' - became a crime.

- Until 1967, it was still illegal to be homosexual in the UK, and people could be imprisoned for it.

- Abortion was illegal until 1968.

- For many years, smoking was permitted in public places. However, on July 1, 2007, a smoking ban in England went into effect, making it illegal to smoke in all enclosed workplaces in England. The ban was due to the proven health risks and diseases caused by smoking and secondary smoke to non-smokers. Astonishingly, alcohol is not banned even though it also causes diseases and harms non-drinkers, i.e. drunk driving.

- The European Court of Human Rights ruled in 2002 that transgender people's right to privacy, as well as their right to marry and start a family, were violated by UK law. According to the judges, the UK government should help trans people by issuing new birth certificates that reflect their gender identity and allowing them to marry someone of the opposite gender. For the first time, lawmakers were forced to recognise their gender identity and the right to the same liberties as everyone else.

- In the past, the sale of pornographic images used to be illegal. But now it has become acceptable in Europe and the US.

Some may argue that it is beneficial for laws to adapt to changing public behaviour; laws should not be set in stone. They should evolve as people's likes and dislikes evolve. But do you believe that rules based on the whims and desires of privileged legislators will result in a safe and equal society for all?

There is a widespread belief that Islamic rules are more draconion. In fact, governments in the U. K. and the U. S. have greater control and monitoring of citizens' actions than ever before.

'In June 2013, the US whistle-blower Edward Snowden revealed that the US and the UK security services are routinely collecting, processing and storing vast quantities of global digital communications, including email messages, posts and private messages on social networks, internet histories, and phone calls. The UK government hasn't publicly accepted that these mass-spying programmes exist' Amnesty International. Isn't this the kind of control and burden you object to in Islam? It's just that people make the rules you follow instead of Allah.

You have been blessed with the intelligence to know that, unlike humans, Allah is perfect. His laws are not biased toward gender or race. Allah created all humans. We know He loves us, cares for us, meets our needs, and knows what is best for us. In the Hadith Nawawi, the Prophet (saw) said:

'Verily, Allah the Almighty has laid down fara'id (religious obligations), so do not neglect them. He has set boundaries, so do not overstep them. He has prohibited some things, so do not violate them; about some things, He was silent on, out of compassion for you, not forgetfulness, so seek not after them.'

Some non-Muslims frequently will make you feel Islamic laws are too difficult and that you should have a choice whether you stick to them. A classic example is wearing hijab. They will say, 'Hijab is oppressive!' and no one (God or your parents) can tell you what to wear. Your body, your choice'. They apply the liberal principle of 'anything is okay if by choice, but not if forced'.

If you were asked why do you or Muslim women wear hijab? What would you say? We don't want people to think we are weak and submissive, so it's easier to say 'I choose to wear the hijab' than 'I wear the hijab because it's obligatory. As a Muslim, this is what Allah wants me to do.' It is important to note that choice is not a fundamentally incorrect motivation in Islam. By being Muslim, you have submitted to the Will of Allah, and you agree to abide by His rules unconditionally.

If a person doesn't believe in Allah and the Prophet Muhammad (saw), they won't understand the idea of submission, paradise and hell, or reward and punishment in the next life. However, to be Muslim is to submit one's personal choices and fleeting desires to the choices Allah has made for us and to align our will with His.

Allah has made many things permissible in this world and forbidden other things. In the following chapters, let's look at what teenagers are being encouraged to experiment with, such as drugs, alcohol, sex and LGBTQIA+, and what is the Islamic perspective on them.

WHY ARE DRUGS AND ALCOHOL HARAM?

Your parents and teachers will warn you against using drugs and drinking alcohol. They are harmful to your health. You may become reliant on them. So why do so many people take them if they're so bad?

How do they work?

When you're doing something you enjoy, your brain produces dopamine, a neurotransmitter. Neurotransmitters are chemical messengers that your body can't function without. Their job is to carry chemical signals (messages) from one neuron (nerve cell) to the next target cell, which can be another nerve cell, a muscle cell or a gland.

All over your brain, receptors grab these chemicals as they float around, increasing your sense of pleasure. These receptors become more sensitive during adolescence. Drugs can bind to these receptors and make you feel good, like you're on top of the world: until they wear off. This pleasurable feeling or 'high' is usually followed by a period when you feel much worse; this is known as a comedown.

Alcohol binds to other receptors in your brain; it reduces inhibitions, making you feel more confident and do things you'll regret once you're sober. It also affects the part of your brain responsible for balance and coordination, making you clumsy. A large amount of alcohol can make you sick and even kill you.

Is cannabis harmless?

There are many different types of drugs, such as cocaine and heroin, but I'm going to concentrate on the most popular recreational drug used by young people worldwide: cannabis. Cannabis, also known as marijuana, dope, or weed, has grown in popularity since the 1960s.

Cannabis is illegal in every Muslim country, the United Kingdom, and most US states. Still, according to a 2017 poll, nearly half (45%) of Americans have tried marijuana at some point.[15] According to a 2018 study, 15% of Americans used marijuana in the previous year.

Marijuana, aside from its revolting odour, is associated with several adverse physical and psychological effects. In February 2015, a team of researchers at King's College London's Institute of Psychiatry, led by Dr Marta Di Forti, discovered that using high-potency cannabis, known as skunk, increased the risk of psychosis by three times when compared to non-use. [16]

Psychosis is a mental disorder that causes difficulty distinguishing between what is real and what is not. Symptoms may include delusions and hallucinations, incoherent speech, and inappropriate behaviour. Sleep issues, social withdrawal, a lack of motivation, and difficulties carrying out daily activities are also possible. The study of 780 people also discovered that those who used cannabis daily were five times more likely to develop psychosis.

The critical question is, why do people smoke weed? Research studies found that the top four primary motives were curiosity and experimentation, fun and peer acceptance.[17]

Some people are drawn to intoxicants that appear exciting, such as smoking marijuana or other stronger drugs, drinking alcohol, or hanging out with people who do those things. It is also regarded as an act of rebellion against parents and authority.

Moreover, drug dealers are cunning; they target young people who they see as easy prey. Because teenagers are more likely to trust someone their own age, older drug dealers recruit young people to sell drugs to them. It's also important to remember that criminals who manufacture and sell illegal drugs cannot be trusted. This means it's impossible to know exactly what is in the white powder you're snorting. The drugs could have also been mixed with hazardous chemicals.

When you have less control over your thoughts and behaviour due to drugs or alcohol, you may find yourself in dangerous situations with no awareness or ability to protect yourself from having photos taken of you or being raped. When you are vulnerable, immoral men or women will take advantage of you. The author of Asking For It, Louise O'Neill, remarks how common this is 'All of my friends have stories of sexual assault and sexual experiences that weren't right. They'll say this is what happened when I was 17, and the terrible thing is I'm not surprised. I'm not surprised that they were sexually assaulted or raped, that their drinks were spiked, or they were too drunk to consent.'[18]

Substance abuse may worsen mental health conditions such as depression or anxiety, and users may be more likely to develop mental illness. People who regularly use drugs or alcohol may feel unable to function without them, and their lives may revolve around obtaining more. The drug then takes control of them, making addiction difficult to overcome.

You may have an image in your mind of a drug dealer: a non-Muslim man wearing a hoodie, looking scary, swearing, and selling drugs in a dark alley. That is not always accurate. It's a sad fact that there are Muslim drug dealers. They don't care that Allah has clearly stated in the

Quran that taking or selling intoxicating substances is haram.

'O You who believe! Intoxicants and gambling, (dedication of) stones and (divination by) arrows are an abomination of Satan's handiwork. Avoid (such abominations) that you may prosper.' (Al-Ma'idah, 5:90)

Or the hadith of Umm Salamah narrated, *'The Prophet (saw) prohibited anything which makes a person drunk or feeble (or causes numbness to the brain).' (Ahmad)*

What does a drug dealer look like?

Drug dealers come in all shapes and sizes. They can be young or old. Male or female. They can wear topis or hijabs. Friends sell them to their classmates, and uncles have no problems telling their adolescent nephews and nieces to sell them to their mates at school. One thing they all have in common is that they are more concerned with making money than with the welfare of their unsuspecting 'customers'. They remind me of vampires, sucking the life out of their victims.

Selling drugs is a lucrative business. Stacey Dooley, an investigative journalist for the BBC, spoke to schoolchildren as young as 15 who claimed they could make £300 a day using fake profiles on Instagram and Snapchat in a programme titled, 'Kids Selling Drugs Online'. However, don't believe the hype, the life of a drug dealer is fraught with danger. Fear of being arrested and thrown into jail. Fear of being stabbed by rival drug dealers. Always looking over their shoulder wondering who will get them first...

So, what underhand tactics do young drug dealers employ? Here are some of the most common scenarios that you may encounter:

- Someone will approach you and offer you a 'free' joint. The aim is to get you hooked so that you will become a regular customer.

- If you are stressed about your exams or feeling sad, a 'friend' will suggest smoking a joint to help you relax and forget about your problems.

- A 'good-looking' guy will begin to show interest in you and lavish you with compliments and attention. Once he has your trust, he will offer you a joint and say, 'It's harmless; everyone does it.' 'Don't be such a killjoy, just chill', he will say, 'I won't tell anyone.' When you are not looking, he will take a photo of you smoking so he can use it for blackmail later. Once he knows you are addicted: he has you under his control. He will start charging you for the drugs. He will tell you that you can pay by having sex with him or pimping you out to his friends if you cannot pay. If you do not comply, he will threaten to send photos of you smoking with him to your family. And this is how young harami drug dealers deceive unsuspecting girls into a life of drug addiction.

You may believe that only 'bad girls or stupid girls' use drugs and get into trouble, but this is not the case. You may think I am exaggerating, but I am not. I'm writing from my experience as a high school teacher and sharing narratives from my students, teenage children and nephews.

I'm not telling you this to scare you. I'm writing to let you know that people like this exist. I want you to understand how to protect yourself. This information is important because knowledge is power. In these cases, it is the ability to protect yourself from harm.

The pull of alcohol

Alcohol is just as bad as drugs, and because it is legal and cheap to buy (in non-Muslim countries) and so enticingly advertised, it is very easy to begin drinking. However, the following real-life experience of a convert sister provides a more realistic picture of what it's like to become addicted to alcohol.

'I was addicted to alcohol. It wasn't because I liked drinking; it's because being drunk made me forget the things that made me sad and anxious. I drank to calm my nerves in social situations or because I didn't know how to say no. Or maybe because I felt I couldn't say no. Additionally, if I became embarrassed in public or anything, drinking was my way out. Right before you lose your balance and your inhibitions, being intoxicated is like being at a carnival.

When I was drinking, my tongue was looser, and my jokes funnier. I was the life of the party. I sucked up the oxygen in the room until there wasn't anymore. And then I kept going. It's as though my stomach was bottomless. I drank until a trapdoor opened, and all the contents of my stomach dropped out onto the floor, along with the bile and my guts. It's a painful experience. But then, so is alcoholism.' Karen Michelle Kaiser.[19]

Alcohol consumption causes many problems; drunk driving kills people, domestic violence and sexual assault, to name a few. Have you ever wondered why alcohol is not illegal in non-Muslim countries when it causes more harm than good?

Should drugs be legalised?

You may be surprised to learn that Germany, Europe's largest economy, will soon join Canada and the state of California in legalising cannabis for recreational use. This could create momentum to change the UN convention restricting plant cultivation and pressure neighbouring European states to follow Germany's lead.

With an estimated annual domestic demand of 400 tonnes of cannabis, economists predict Germany will gain approximately £4 billion per year in additional tax receipts and cost savings from no longer prosecuting those who enjoy a spliff or two. The government's official motivation for legalisation is to break up the illegal cannabis trade, allowing it to control the quality of cannabis on the market, prevent the spread of contaminated substances, and protect minors.

Sadiq Khan, the Mayor of London, is investigating the possibility of decriminalising cannabis. Khan stated that he believed it would help 'tackle drug-related crime, protect Londoners' health, and reduce the huge damage that illegal drugs cause to our communities.' He added, 'The illegal drug trade causes huge damage to our society, and we need to do more to tackle this epidemic and further the debate around our drug laws.'[20]

People advocate for the legalisation of recreational drug use for a variety of reasons.

- They believe in personal freedom and that as long as they are not causing harm to others, it is acceptable to consume drugs (even illegal ones) and alcohol in moderation.

- Politicians and law enforcement agencies know that many people use drugs and believe the situation is out of control. Even politicians have admitted to using illegal drugs. Traces of cocaine were discovered in the Houses of Parliament during a recent investigation.[21]

- If drugs are legalised, the government can tax sellers and spend less money prosecuting and imprisoning people. The quality of the drugs can also be checked.

But how does this affect Muslims? Is it okay for us to start smoking cannabis if it becomes legal? What about simply selling it and not using it? When it comes to alcohol, many Muslim-owned restaurants do precisely that! But we do not change our rules because some Muslims choose to disobey Allah (swt). Politicians make the laws in liberal secular societies, so lawmakers will change the rules if public opinion changes. More and more countries may legalise drugs in the future.

As Muslims, we are aware that Allah's laws are the best. So we do not ignore Allah's law to seek pleasure or have a side hustle selling drugs. Muslims who obtain their rizq (provision) by selling alcohol and drugs will have no barakah (blessings) from their wealth, and they will be punished in the next life.

The Messenger of Allah (saw) said, *'Allah the Almighty is Good and accepts only that which is good. And verily Allah has commanded the believers to do that which He has commanded the Messengers. So the Almighty has said: 'O (you) Messengers! Eat of the tayyibat [all kinds of halal (legal) foods], and perform righteous deeds.' (Al-Mu'minun,23:51) and the Almighty has said: 'O you who believe! Eat of the lawful things that We have provided you.' (Al-Baqarah,2:172)' Then he (saw) mentioned [the case] of a man who, having journeyed far, is dishevelled and dusty, and who spreads out his hands to the sky saying 'O Lord! O Lord!,' while his food is haram (unlawful), his drink is haram, his clothing is haram, and he has been nourished with haram, so how can [his supplication] be answered?' (Muslim)*

When Allah forbids something, we must trust that Allah knows what is best for us. That is our test. Allah, the Almighty says,
'And it may be that you dislike a thing which is good for you and that you like a thing which is bad for you. Allah knows, but you do not know.' (Al-Baqarah, 2:216)

Which types of drugs are prohibited in Islam?

Ibn Umar reported that Allah's Messenger said, *'Every intoxicant is khamr (wine), and every intoxicant is haram (unlawful). Whosoever drinks wine in this world and dies whilst consumed in it and does not repent will not drink it in the next world.' (Muslim).*

Remember that when the term intoxicant is used, it also includes narcotics because they cause a loss of self-control. As a result, all intoxicants are considered haram due to their inebriant repercussions and their physical-mental adverse effects on individuals and families. Furthermore, drug use degrades morals, corrupts the body and mind, causes severe cultural, social, and economic losses, and ruins societies. Unfortunately, many young women sell their bodies to support their drug addiction.

A drug addict cannot control their behaviour, loses motivation and common sense, and is willing to do anything to obtain drugs without hesitation. They cannot fully adhere to their Islamic practises because drugs make them irresponsible. Allah warns us that:

'Shaytan's plan is to sow hatred and enmity amongst you with intoxicants and gambling. And to hamper you from the remembrance of Allah and from prayer. Will you not give up?' (Al-Maidah, 5:91)

Sometimes, you may act impulsively, take risks, and have poor judgement and insight. As a result, you may be more inclined to experiment with alcohol and drugs. To impress your friends, you may do things you would not normally do or regret later.

Your values and boundaries are based on Islam; do not be forced to do anything you do not want to do. You are accountable to Allah for your actions; if something goes wrong, you alone will face the consequences, even if your peers cheer you on. Substances are sometimes used to mask complicated feelings such as loneliness, anxiety and sadness rather than find healthy ways to cope. They only deliver a temporary solution to an ordeal you are facing. If you believe this is the case for you, speak to someone who can help.

If you've made a mistake and taken drugs or alcohol, that doesn't mean you can't change or that you should let it define who you are. Everyone makes mistakes. Sincerely, do dua to Allah, and ask Him to forgive you and help you. Don't continue indulging in the sin further. Stop hanging out with friends who smoke weed or drink alcohol. Just stop. Make a conscious decision and effort to quit this wrongdoing immediately. If you think you are addicted to a substance and you are unable to stop on your own, then you must speak to your family and seek medical help. I know that won't be easy to do but with the right help and support, you can get drug or alcohol-free and stay that way.

We cannot be sinless, but we can restrain ourselves by controlling our nafs (lower self), cleansing our thoughts and acts, performing good actions, choosing decent friends who encourage us to obey Allah, and asking Allah for forgiveness. It was narrated from Anas that the Messenger of Allah (saw) said:

'Every son of Adam commits sin, and the best of those who commit sin are those who repent.' (Sunan Ibn Majah)

Sometimes we feel trapped by our sins. We don't think we're worthy of seeking forgiveness but remembering this is Shaytan's trick for you to begin doubting Allah's mercy and fall deeper into your sin. If you were soiled with filth, would you not take a shower to cleanse yourself? Or would you think you're too dirty for a shower? Allah is Al Ghaffar; the Most Forgiving. What's beautiful about this name is that Allah is telling us that He will readily forgive and cover up the sins we cannot even forgive ourselves for. So, there's always hope.[22]

THERE IS NOTHING FUN ABOUT PORNOGRAPHY

P ornography is the representation of people in books, pictures, statues, films, and other media with little or no clothing. It also includes people exhibiting sexual behaviour. Looking at it can cause many feelings simultaneously: disgust, excitement and curiosity.

Pornography shows the parts of the body that we keep private. Allah created our bodies, so every aspect of our body is good, including our private parts, but taking pictures of them and showing them to others is unacceptable; it's haram. For your safety, keep your private parts private. Most juveniles who see pornography know instantly that it feels wrong or weird. Some say it makes them feel embarrassed or even sick to their stomachs. Unfortunately, studies show that watching online pornography is considered normal by some teenagers.[23] So why do some teenagers look at it?

Pornography is problematic because it's designed to feel exciting to your body. Pornography deceives the brain into releasing a large dose of chemicals, dopamine[24], that make your body feel good for a short time. But this can quickly lead to porn addiction because you keeping craving the dopamine hit. The problem is that pornography can hurt parts of your developing brain.[25] Looking at pornography is dangerous. So why do even young kids find it so easily online if it is so bad?

The pornography industry is worth billions.[26] It is widely available online, so many kids accidentally see it on computers, phones, tablets etc. Sometimes kids are shown pornography by a friend or family member. Has that ever happened to you? No one should ever show pornography to you. If that ever happens, you should tell an adult that you trust.

So why do teens want to look at pornography?

It's normal for teenagers to be curious about sex and relationships, and some teens become curious about pornography. Sometimes they may search online for information or answers to questions they have. They may do this if they're worried or embarrassed about asking their parents or guardians. Some of the reasons children and young people watch or search for porn online include:

- to learn about sex and sexual identity
- for sexual arousal and pleasure
- curiosity
- for a laugh
- break the rules
- to be disgusted
- to freak out their friend
- peer or relationship pressure [27]

For many, wanting to see pornography can feel like the pull of a giant magnet. After seeing only one pornographic picture, their brains can be deceived into wanting to see more and more. But, like I said previously, pornography damages your mind.

How does pornography damage your mental health?

Grammy-winning singer Billie Eilish has spoken about her addiction to watching pornography, starting at age 11, and how it gave her nightmares and messed her up when she began dating.

'I think porn is a disgrace. I used to watch a lot of porn, to be honest. I started watching porn when I was, like, 11.' It made her feel as if she was cool and 'one of the guys...I think it really destroyed my brain and I feel incredibly devastated that I was exposed to so much porn,' she added, saying she suffered nightmares because some of the content she watched was so violent and abusive. Eilish said she is now angry at herself for thinking it was okay to watch so much pornography. 'The first few times I, you know, had sex, I was not saying no to things that were not good. It was because I thought that's what I was supposed to be attracted to.' [28]

According to an NSPCC survey of more than 1000 young people aged 11 to 16 in 2017: [29]

- 44% of boys said that pornography had given them ideas about the type of sex they wanted to try, compared to 29% of girls.
- 48% of 11 to 16-year-olds had seen pornography online.
- 28% of 11 to 12-year-olds reported having seen pornography, though none of the girls claimed they had actively searched for it; more boys have watched online pornography than girls.

There are three ways that pornography damages you. Young people who watch porn or sexually explicit content are at greater risk of developing:

- Unrealistic expectations of body image and performance.
- Unrealistic attitudes about sex and consent.
- More negative attitudes about roles and identities in relation-ships.

Pornography teaches that a person's body is an object to use instead of a whole person who deserves to be loved and respected. The people in pornographic images are all actors all the images presented to viewers are fantasy. They do not look like 'normal' people. They wear a lot of make-up. Many have plastic surgery to enhance their bodies. The men take steroids to make their muscles look more prominent.

When people see others as sexualised objects, it's much easier to mistreat them. Many women and children are forced to take part in the production of pornography. They have no choice. No safeguards or checks are being carried out on pornography websites. Anyone can upload images, and anyone,
including children, can easily view these degrading and vile images.

Secondly, pornography teaches men it's okay to hurt women! It shows men physically abusing women, but the women act like it's fun. So young women begin to think it's acceptable for a man to mistreat them. The third way pornography can hurt a person's brain is that looking at it can become a bad habit or even a severe addiction.

What is addiction?
You may have heard people say they are addicted to chocolate or tea. However, real addiction is a severe problem. People whose lives are taken over by addictions are called addicts. An addiction is like a powerful habit so intense that most addicts can't quit, even when they have tried hard to stop. It feels like a trap they can't escape. For example, people can be addicted to smoking or alcohol or drugs. People can also become addicted to behaviours like scrolling on their phones or looking at pornography. Some people become addicted more easily than others. But you never want to become addicted to anything.

Most addicts make bad choices that end up hurting themselves and their loved ones. They often try to hide their addiction by lying to their friends and family. As they become increasingly addicted, they lose interest in their family and friends. But, if pornography is so harmful to adults and young people, why is it legal?

In Europe, the US, and Australia, pornography is legal for adults to view because they believe in individual freedom. The only restriction on personal liberty is that you should not cause harm to another person. The argument is that if the porn actors, men and women, are in control of what is being done to them, they are getting paid, and they enjoy it, then it is okay. Also, no one should judge or dictate to people what they can watch as long as they do not harm anyone; it's their choice. Surprisingly, many feminists also agree with this view, even though women have significantly suffered due to the commercialisation of sex through the insidious pornography industry.[30]

For Muslims, the cure to the disease of pornography and all forms of 'sex work' is a no-brainer: zero tolerance. Islam puts so much emphasis on respecting and honouring women. The idea of using your body to make money is alien to Islam. But in the movie Hustlers, self-proclaimed feminist Jennifer Lopez glamorises the act of stripping in front of men for money. 'There's something liberating and empowering about it, but you're really out there, physically, emotionally and psychologically.' [31]

It defies logic for many feminists who regard pornography as sexist to consider its censorship harmful. It's a phenomenon that reveals more nakedly than ever before the true face of feminism.This is because prohibiting pornography contradicts their unflinching belief in individualism. But Islam does not believe that an individual's rights supersede the well-being of the wider community. It's rather the opposite, as illustrated by the following hadith:

Al-Nu'man ibn Bashir reported: The Prophet (saw) said, 'The parable of those who respect the limits of Allah and those who violate them is that of people who board a ship after casting lots, some of them residing in its upper deck and others in its lower deck. When those in the lower deck want water, they pass by the upper deck and say: If we tear a hole in the bottom of the ship, we will not harm those above us. If those in the upper deck let them do what they want, they will all be destroyed together. If they restrain them, they will all be saved together.; (Bukhāri)

Therefore, Allah has made all types of 'sex work' haram, such as prostitution. Jabir reported: that Abdullah ibn Ubayy would say to his servant girl, *'Go earn us something from prostitution.'* Then, Allah Almighty revealed, *'Do not compel your slave girls to prostitution if they desire chastity, seeking thereby the interests of worldly life. If someone compels them, Allah is forgiving and merciful to them after their compulsion.' (An-Nur,24:33) (Muslim)*

For our good, Allah says: *'Tell the believing men to lower their gaze (from looking at forbidden things) and to protect their private parts (from illegal sexual acts, etc.). That is purer for them. Verily, Allah is All-Aware of what they do." (An-Nur, 24:30)*

And the Prophet (saw) said: *'The adultery of the eyes is by looking' (i.e. by looking at what Allah has forbidden). (Bukhari)*

Pornography is not a bit of fun or victimless. So an Islamic government would stop the production of pornography and severely punish those who make, distribute, and consume it. Anyone who genuinely cares about the well-being of women would agree with the Islamic ruling and call for a complete ban. Improving working conditions or legalising the sex industry, a solution proposed by some, will not stop women from being humiliated and degraded.

PROM STRESS

Prom night and after parties are complex for some Muslims because it involves guys and girls dancing, revealing dresses, the certainty of alcohol and drugs and the expectation of sex. For others, it's a rite of passage. I'm sure you have an opinion or haven't made up your mind, and I'm here to unpack the arguments. So, let's take a closer look at the whole 'Prom' thing.

Prom Distraction

Proms take place in the senior year of high school. Your final year is stressful because you have exams to prepare for. You're putting in long hours, spending hours researching topics. If you care about your future and are doing these things: you have your priorities straight. But what if you're not trawling over quadratic equations or researching genetic engineering but agonising over which prom dress to buy or spending hours on TikTok looking at hairstyles and dance moves?

Why do high schools encourage students to devote so much time and energy to a frivolous party when they are about to take their final year exams? Unfortunately, every high school student has been led to believe that prom is this magical evening watching movies where the unpopular geek is transformed into the most glamorous girl in school, and 16-year-old girls feel like Bella Hadid sauntering down the red carpet with all eyes on them!

Prom, unheard of in the United Kingdom 20 years ago, is now the 'highlight' of the year for thousands of school leavers. Excessive 'passing out' celebrations for Year 11 students (aged 15-16) and Year 13 students (aged 17-18) have become the norm, causing untold anxiety for students and financial hardship for parents. More than 85% of British schools now hold school proms - in the US, it's 95%- which range from boat parties to custom-made extravaganzas!

The average cost of Prom night

Naive high schoolers become enveloped in extravagant fantasy, and unsuspecting parents are happy to foot the bill in the name of their child's happiness. The price of a single night of prom 'fun' is shocking. According to a Visa survey, the average American family spent $919 per attendee on prom night in 2015. And Promaholics.com, a site dedicated to 'All things prom,' 'Choosing a prom dress is up there with choosing a wedding dress.' Go-Compare stated the average cost for a UK parent in 2015 was £190, representing a 23 per cent increase since 2013.

When I was teaching at a high school, Muslim parents would typically spend £150 on a dress, £120 on a 5-seater limousine, £35 on makeup, and £50 on shoes! It's no surprise that the UK high school prom industry is worth £90 million annually. Expensive proms create a cycle of teenagers constantly trying to outdo each other, increasing the cost of the evenings. No parent should be emotionally blackmailed into paying £120 an hour for a limousine that they won't get the pleasure of sitting in.

The Prom Fantasy

The allure and distinctive red carpet look linked with proms stem from a lifelong diet of teen movies and shows and a money-oriented world in which schoolgirls and boys compare themselves to film stars and footballers. Proms incite celebrity fantasy by allowing teenagers to pretend to be movie stars for the evening. Something is very wrong here.

Exam stress, as we all know, is a necessary evil; prom stress, on the other hand, is a headache you should avoid. As I previously stated, I am a high school teacher, and GCSEs and A-levels (the final year exams in the UK) have become increasingly difficult to pass. As a result, students must dedicate more time and energy to their studies. Consequently, it makes no sense for schools to encourage students to waste, yes, waste, time after school organising prom bake sales.

It's no wonder that UK students are stuck in the educational doldrums, according to the influential PISA report. The Programme for International Student

Assessment (PISA) is undertaken once every three years and tests 15-year-olds' abilities in the core academic disciplines of Reading, Maths and Science. Launched in 2000, around 540,000 students from 72 countries took part in PISA in 2015. The UK results were abysmal: Science 15th place, Reading 21st and Maths 27th. Do you think the parents of high school students in Singapore, China or Finland (these countries were in the top 10 rankings) would let their kids squander their time a few months before their GCSE exams?

Is it haram to go to a school dance?

As you may have guessed, my daughter did not attend her school prom, nor did her older brother. And it's not because I'm a stingy scrooge. Having studied the ayah and hadith about socialising in Islam. I can't find any Islamic evidence that teenagers who have reached puberty (who no longer see themselves as 'school kids') can attend a mixed party while looking absolutely stunning (with or without hijab) and where couples will be dancing, flirting, and kissing. Every Muslim knows that having a girlfriend, boyfriend, or prom date (even for one night) is forbidden.

As we all know, Islam is a way of life. As such, it has comprehensive social laws that regulate the relationship between men and women, aiming to direct and restrict the fulfilment of sexual desires to marriage alone. These social rules also include the Islamic dress code (for both genders), the prohibition of an unrelated man and woman being alone, and the prohibition of non-essential gender mixing and intimate relationships outside marriage. These laws have a tangible, positive impact on society by protecting both genders from predators, protecting the family unit and children's rights, and ensuring productive, desexualised interaction between men and women that are not cheapened or belittled by one night stands.

Are mixed school dances allowed in Islam?

When the Prophet (saw) saw men and women mingling as they left the masjid, he ordered them to separate. He even created separate entrances for the genders within the mosque to ensure separation. He (saw) also organised separate classes for men and women to learn about Islam. To prevent men and women from mixing during prayers, the Messenger (saw) arranged them into separate lines, and the women would leave the mosque before the men.Umm Salamah, the wife of the Prophet (saw), narrated, *'Whenever Allah's Apostle completed the prayer with Taslim, the women used to get up immediately, and Allah's Apostle would remain at his place and so would the men who prayed with him.' (Bukhari)*

This evidence establishes the general norm in Islam is that men and women are obliged to be separate. Still, there are clear exceptions prescribed by the Qur'an and Sunnah where they are permitted to meet and interact for a clearly defined purpose – for example, in education, eating, seeking medical care, trade, accounting the ruler, raising their political opinions within society. Hence, gender separation is a well-known and essential Islamic tradition that is part of everyday life within Muslim communities practised in mosques, Muslim institutions, and homes.

Do not approach zina

Zina (adultery, fornication) refers to more than just the physical act; there is also zina of the hand, which is touching what is forbidden, and zina of the eyes, which is looking at what is forbidden. Some people justify going to prom by saying, 'I'll be at a table with only my (Muslim) friends, and I won't dance with any boys.' But, let's be honest, what do you expect to see other couples doing at a prom? What kind of music will the DJ play? What will everyone be talking about?

It was narrated from Abu Hurayrah that the Prophet (saw) said: *'Allah has decreed for every son of Adam his share of zina, which he will inevitably commit. The zina of the eyes is looking, the zina of the tongue is speaking, one may wish and desire, and the private parts confirm that or deny it.' (Bukhari & Muslim)*

It is not permissible for a Muslim to long for the things that lead to zina, such as kissing, being alone, touching and looking, for all these things are haram and lead to the greater evil: zina.Allah says:

'And come not near to unlawful sex. Verily, it is a Faahishah (i.e. anything that transgresses its limits: a great sin, and an evil way that leads one to hell unless Allah forgives them)' (Al-Isra' 17:32)

One of the arrows of, Shaytan is looking at what is forbidden, which leads a person to shamelessness, even if they did not do it intentionally at first. Allah says:

'Tell the believing men to lower their gaze (from looking at forbidden things) and protect their private parts (from illegal sexual acts). That is purer for them. Verily, Allah is All-Aware of what they do.'

'And tell the believing women to lower their gaze (from looking at forbidden things), and protect their private parts (from illegal sexual acts)' (Al-Noor 24:30-31)

Think about how Allah connects the issue of lowering the gaze with the issue of protecting the private parts (guarding one's chastity) in these verses and how lowering the gaze is mentioned first before protecting the private parts because the eye influences the heart.

Muslim prom dress?

I know you face immense pressure to follow the crowd, and it doesn't help when your Muslim friends are all going. They'll say, 'It's just a harmless school party? It's the last time we'll all be together! There won't be any alcohol, and the food will be halal.' But that mindset shows that they think Islam is just a bunch of dietary rules. Fame-hungry, Muslim YouTubers create 'How to hijabify your prom dress' and 'Get ready with me for Prom: turban tutorial' Why are Muslims so keen to ape non-Muslims?

We don't want to be like the people mentioned in the ayah:

'And leave alone those who take their religion as play and amusement and are deceived by the life of this world. But remind (them) with it (the Quran) lest a person be given up to destruction for that which he has earned, when he will find for himself no protector or intercessor besides Allah, and even if he offers every ransom, it will not be accepted from him. Such are they who are given up to destruction because of that which they have earned' (Al-An'am 6:70)

Today it's a high school prom; tomorrow, it will be a friends house warming party; as a god-fearing Muslimah, you must avoid events and parties that you know will lure you into doing something contrary to Islam. As the Holy Qur'an puts it so exquisitely:

'The one who does a bad deed shall be recompensed to the extent of the bad deed done; and the one who is a believer and does good deeds, whether man or woman, shall enter Paradise and therein receive sustenance without measure.' (Al-Ghafir, 40:40)

As you leave high school, you are at a crossroads; you are moving from the re-strictions of school to the freedom of college. It's a delicate time; you're at the cusp of adulthood, and to make the right choices, you need to follow Islamic guidance. While prom may seem like the be-all, end-all of events for you at the moment, inshallah, soon it will be a distant memory...

In Allah's eternal gardens, there is an awe-inspiring party full of boundless things beyond your wildest dreams. So, you have a choice between a one-night party that will usually not live up to expectations at your high school or an eter-nal party in paradise beyond your wildest imagination. Which will you choose?

BROKEN HEARTS

Zaynab Mufti

They say broken hearts heal with time
So, I'm staring at the clock waiting for mine
It's a waiting game, and I feel kind of lame
But I'm watching the hands move
Because I no longer have anything left to lose
Because he doesn't love me anymore
Every time I try see him, he shuts the door
I'm telling you, he doesn't love me anymore

I gave up my days for him
Sat up all night played games with him
Left all I had and gave to him every thought, word, and action
Yes, sometimes, I'll admit I used him as a distraction
But. honestly, it was mainly attraction

I did sometimes feel forced because eyes were on me
People around me expected it of me
We were a power pair
When we were together, it was like Chuck and Blair
Ah, I could swear
If only you knew

I gave up my time for him
Left my prayers behind for him
Got excited and committed crimes for him
Told myself it was worth it
Those moments of happiness, I deserved it
But he doesn't love me anymore

Really, I can tell you for sure
He doesn't love me anymore

You know that one day it hit me, I'll remember till the day I die
When I realised that I was the victim and he was the bad guy
Nah, I don't cry
I don't show emotion I'm a tough guy
But this one broke me
He took my heart, made me think I was happy, and then choked me
His hands around my neck like a noose
He played me and then let me loose
Pretended to give me the world and then just like that
Took it all away, and then he said to me, 'Pat pat'
He sat me down and said, 'I'll tell you the truth
I broke your heart and made you waste your youth
But it was my duty
You see long ago I made a promise to blind you with beauty
I requested permission to take you off track
Make you bend your back
And give me everything you had
 And every time you try and bounce back
I won't cut you any slack
I want to see you shattered
Down on your knees with all your morals battered
Because you were easy
I flashed you one follower, and you looked at me all cheesy
You were naïve
I splashed you some money, and my goals were achieved
I gave you the fast cars and the music

I gave you TV shows that were exclusive

I made you waste your time till you thought I was too sick

I had you in my grasp, it was simple to hold you in my clasp

'I made you leave your lifeline, your book, for me

I made you constantly look for me

I gave you a taste of my world, and you were hooked to me

It's not my fault you couldn't see the signs

Not my fault you ignored the guidelines

And put down your blinds to the truth that was desperately calling your name

You see, I am merely a game

Nothing but delusion

I cause you confusion and make you come to the wrong conclusions

You thought you loved me

I'm sorry to say, but you misjudged me

I am not your Chuck, and you are not my Blair; I'll be truthful I don't care

My respite comes to an end when the horn is blown

Back to hell, I'll be thrown, all alone

Not going to lie; I just didn't want to be lonely

I was trying to make this world seem homely

So, I broke your heart and made you leave what you've been taught

You sold your soul to me and let yourself be bought

I encouraged you and put you in a trance

Just because I know you still have a chance

Even though you turned your back on Him and gave all your love to me,

God will still welcome you back with open arms
I'm not sorry I broke your heart
I'll keep trying till the day you depart
So, it's a bye for now, but I'll see you soon'
He left the room   ·

He does not love me anymore
My heart is broken, and I'm feeling sore
But at least I know reality
He doesn't love me, and he never did

They say broken hearts heal with time
I don't think I believe in that line
I don't think I'll wait for the hour to pass or for the sand to fall
Maybe all it takes is pulling out the mat and not even giving it my all
Just take a step towards the Almighty and witness Him come running
Move to Him by the length of a hand, and He'll come to me by the
length of an arm
I guess trying won't do me any harm

My ex has been baited
That love was overrated
They say broken hearts heal with time
I no longer believe in that paradigm.

Poem Inspiration - *He said, 'My Lord! since You made me go astray, I
swear that I shall beautify for them (evils) on the earth, and shall lead all
of them astray, Except those of Your servants from among them who are
chosen (by You)' (Surah al-Hijr, verse 39-40)*

FEMINISM EXPLAINED

W hy are Muslims so obsessed with feminism? Male You-Tubers make 'The Danger of Feminism' click-bait videos, whilst female Youtubers push back with 'Islam is a feminist religion.' Muslim Twitter is no better. Have you ever been branded a feminist simply for calling out discrimination against women? But when men acknowledge they want a wife who can cook, they are accused of being misogynists.

So, how can we resolve this? Let's begin by admitting that feminism has become the dominant view around women's issues. It's the gold standard for women's rights and the pursuit of female empowerment. If you live in the west, most of your female teachers will be feminists; books relating to women's issues and the English literature promote feminism. i.e. Margaret Atwood's, Handmaid's Tale and Carol Anne Duffy's Feminine Gospels. Zendaya and fellow 'girl boss' celebrities promote feminism 'A feminist is a person who believes in the power of women just as much as they believe in the power of anyone else. It's equality, it's fairness, I think it's a great thing to be a part of. '32

So whether you know it or not, your views about personal choice, gender roles, and work are impacted by the core beliefs of liberal feminism, which are liberty, individualism and equality. For some girls, the solution to the oppression or sexism experienced at the hands of family members or the Muslim community is straightforward: become a feminist. Whereas, others see it as a vehicle to achieve their Islamic rights.

Unfortunately, Muslims have an Achilles heel regarding women's rights. It's not good enough to say, 'Allah gave Muslim women rights 1400 years ago' because we don't have an example of a Muslim government that comprehensively gives women access to their God-given rights. Instead of counteracting the Islamophobic propaganda surrounding the place of women in Islam, Muslim governments are part of the problem. They don't give Muslim women justice when harassed, beaten or raped. The death of 22-year-old Mahsa Amini in Iran is a prime example.

It's easy to agree with slogans such as 'My Body My Choice' or 'Khadijah was a feminist' (just because she was a business woman). But before you put your faith in feminism, I would like to invite you to gain a deeper understanding of feminism so you can see that its principles and goals are not in tune with Islam.

Feminism comes in many forms. It is often difficult to pin down any clear principles underpinning this ideology because it's constantly evolving. For many, it simply means 'women's rights' – that is, for women to seek rights equal to men. Thus, feminism becomes a form of collective activism calling for equality.

Many Muslim girls observe unfairness within their families and communities in the East and the West, where they are treated reprehensively. The murder of Sadia Manzoor, her daughter and mother in Texas at the hands of her estranged husband, is a heartbreaking example. You only need to look at the unsafe state of the Muslim world to observe injustices, much of which impact women. It's within this context that feminism seems like an appealing idea. To deny these problems and sweep them under the carpet is against the Islamic principle of standing up for justice.

But what is feminism, and how should we understand it? Several waves of feminism have focused on different challenges women face and support diverse aims. Feminism arose from a belief that women were of equal worth to men and thus deserved equal rights. This rights-based culture stems from a liberal value system. Liberalism is an ideology that developed in the seventeenth century in Europe that, within time, would become the frame of thinking embraced by what today we would call 'the West'.

At the root of liberalism is the idea developed by philosopher John Locke that all men were born equal because they were endowed with natural rights. These rights, he argued, were the right to life, liberty and property. Because a king did not grant these, these rights were inalienable and could not be taken away from an individual. Locke's ideas swept through Europe and North America. They contributed to the American and French revolutions, where rights, liberty and equality became the ideals behind these new republics.

But there was a problem with early liberal thinkers. Their recognition of who deserved these rights hinged on who they regarded as fully human and capable of rational thinking. For example, when writing his piece 'On Toleration', Locke saw little contradiction with owning stocks in the Royal African Company, which ran the African slave trade for England. Nor did he feel discomfort with authoring *The Fundamental Constitutions of Carolina* (1669), which states, '*Every freeman of Carolina shall have absolute power and authority over his negro slaves ...*'. This is because black people were viewed as sub-human.

But also, women were infantilised, and their rights to property or autonomy were dependent on men, as it was believed that they were not intelligent enough to make fully thought-through decisions. As these prejudices were challenged, feminism arose out of a desire to expand these natural rights to incorporate women. This desire for liberal equality formed the basis of first-wave feminism. It aimed to achieve equality with men regarding property, education, and legal and voting rights.

First-Wave Feminism

Mary Wollstonecraft was one of the most influential feminist activists and thinkers in the United Kingdom (1759-1797). She argued that rights and equality should be extended to women because they were as rational as men. In eighteenth-century England, women were still not given rights like education and property rights, and she wanted this to be reversed. Muslims would see much of what she campaigned for to be fair regarding access to education and voting rights. Her argument that women are rational beings and thus should not be categorised as children would solicit broad agreement from Muslims. In her seminal work, *A Vindication of the Rights of Women,* she argues,

'My own sex, I hope, will excuse me if I treat them like rational creatures instead of flattering their fascinating graces and viewing them as if they were in a state of perpetual childhood, unable to stand alone.'

Liberal rights to property and liberty did not extend to women simply because they saw them be incapable of managing their own lives. They also thought women were too emotional, lacked cognitive abilities and needed men to help them make sensible decisions. Muslims believe that women are as intelligent as men and deserve to be treated fairly. The Quran clearly states that Allah does not discriminate between genders *'I will never deny any of you—male or female—the reward of your deeds. Both are equal in reward.' (Ali-Imran, 3:195)*

Meaning Allah will judge us equally on the day of judgement based on our deeds. Islam is not sexist. The foundation upon which the Islamic system of law is built is the concept of justice, not equality. *'We have already sent our messengers with clear evidence and sent down with them the scripture and the balance that the people maintain their affairs in justice.' (Al-Hadid,57:25).*

In Islam, we do not believe in the idea that men and women should always have the same (equal) roles and responsibilities. Sometimes they do such as prayer, fasting, and performing hajj are obligatory for both genders. However, Allah created men and women to be different: *'And the male is not like the female.' (Ali-Imran,3:36)* So it is not surprising that Allah, in his wisdom, gave different roles to women and men.

A Muslim woman does not have to do everything a Muslim man does, I.e. it is the duty of Muslim men to be soldiers and fight jihad, but women do not need to, and neither do non-Muslim citizens. Allah gave women absolute property rights, so much so that it would be forbidden for a husband to use his wife's finances on the household expenses unless she willingly accepted to contribute. So equality is not the foundation upon which our marriages and family are built. Interestingly, feminists accept that gender differences exist, but they still stubbornly demand absolute equality. We should not be so irrational.

Wollstonecraft also became disillusioned with the family, which she likened to a prison. This undoubtedly reflected the suffocating dehumanisation of women in her era but would later be adopted by feminists as a cause. For patriarchy to fall, the family had to be dismantled. She also embraced the 'free love' movement, reflected in her personal life. For her, marriage and monogamy were suffocating. If men could have multiple partners, as practised by educated and upper-class men of her time, then women should have the choice to do the same.

Wollstonecraft's views did not reflect that of her society, and it would take another century for women to achieve the public rights she called for. In 1918 in the UK, some women were given the right to vote, which became universal in 1928. This was partly because of the suffragette movement's activism. Female campaigners across Europe and North America would pursue legal and educational rights that characterised first-wave feminism.

Second-Wave Feminism

After achieving the goals set by the suffragette movements in Europe and North America, liberals turned their attention to broader goals. The sexual revolution in the 1960s, prompted partly by the development of the contraceptive pill, created an environment of free love and separated sex from responsibility. Women could now experience a promiscuous life on equal terms to men, where love could be experienced outside the 'oppressive' confines of marriage.

In the USA, the aims of this new feminism crystallised after the publication of Betty Friedan's *The Feminine Mystique*. Friedan referred to the 'feminine mystique as the 'cultural myth' that women sought security and fulfilment in domestic life and 'feminine' behaviour, a myth that discourages women from entering employment, politics and public life in general.

She highlighted what she called 'the problem with no name', by which she meant the sense of despair and deep unhappiness many women experience because they are confined to a domestic existence and are thus unable to gain fulfilment in a career or through political life. She reimagines the American home as a 'comfortable concentration camp.' This critique of the family resonated with many young women, and a new movement was formed.

Second-wave feminism recognised that the legal and political rights that were hard-won by earlier women had not solved the 'women's question.' This transformed the women's movement into a broader social one, where more radical solutions were sought. Books such as Simone de Beauvoir's The Second Sex, Kate Millett's Sexual Politics (1970) and Germaine Greer's The Female Eunuch (1970) pushed back the borders of what had previously been considered 'political' by focusing on the personal, psychological and sexual aspects of female oppression.

Until now, politics is what happened outside the home – these feminists argued that women would never achieve liberation until there was a radical transformation of the family and the dismantling of the patriarchy. This is why what happened in the family was also political and must be the subject of feminist activism.

This new wave of feminism was pro-gay and lesbian and questioned the meaning of 'gender', 'femininity' and 'womanhood'. They believed these terms were not linked to biological sex but socially constructed ideas. In other words, masculine and feminine traits were acquired from society and not part of nature, so your biology does not determine your destiny.

It is simply factually incorrect to declare that 'gender' is entirely a cultural construct with no fundamental link to biological sex. The DNA of the male and female is different, and so women and men are physically, biologically and emotionally not the same.

Equality meant women and men were the same or androgynous, showing neither male nor female qualities. This lack of texture, an ideology of sameness, meant that any social expectations society placed on women were unjust. Millett's book was dubbed a 'bible for feminists', and the 1970s gave rise to several movements demanding abortion on demand, equal pay and state-sponsored childcare.

The 1973 Roe v Wade judgment of the US Supreme Court was a significant victory for second-wave feminist campaigners. Reproductive rights broke one chink in the chain of inequalities. Until now, men could sleep around without consequence, yet women were constrained by motherhood. In *The Dialectic of Sex* (1970), Shulamith Firestone described a world liberated from 'The tyranny of reproduction'. Women were now free from the consequences of relationships.

The disruption of the patriarchy worked to men's advantage. Previously, most men had to sign up for various responsibilities before sex, including financial ones. The post-patriarchal society removed these safeguards to the disadvantage of women.

Not all feminists agreed with these prescriptions; it would be incorrect to present feminism as a uniform movement. Some rightly concluded that the pursuit of equality would mean that women would be 'male-identified'. To be 'equal' meant to aspire to the goals of men. These 'difference feminists' realised that aspiring to be like men would take away feminine qualities and aspirations.

The belief that women and men are fundamentally different at a psycho-biological level meant that women must not aspire to be like men but rather seek liberation through difference and not as 'sexless' persons. Known as the 'pro-woman' movement, there was an emphasis on the qualities women brought to society, empathy, compassion, and the promotion of experiences such as childbirth, motherhood and menstruation.

However, difference feminism has also given rise to a political movement that observes 'all men' as the enemy. If men are predisposed to repressing women, female separatism is the only way forward. Women can retreat to a world where they can be women. For example, Susan Brownmiller's *Against Our Will* (1975) emphasised that men dominate women through a method of physical and sexual abuse. Men have created an 'ideology of rape', which amounts to a 'conscious process of intimidation by which all men keep all women in a state of fear.' Thus to truly find liberation, one must first end the reliance on men.

Heterosexual women are therefore thought to be 'male identified', incapable of fully realising their true nature and becoming 'female identified'. These assumptions led to the development of political lesbianism, which argues that sexual preferences are an issue of crucial political importance for women. Only women who remain celibate or choose lesbianism can regard themselves as 'woman-identified women'. The slogan attributed to

Ti-Grace Atkinson: 'feminism is the theory; lesbianism is the practice', illustrates this point.

Third Wave Feminism

Third Wave Feminism emerged in the 1990s and came out of dissatisfaction with the white-middle-class bias that consumed activists of the previous two stages. It highlights the stories of other black, Asian, poor and less educated women and their struggles. Although the gap between white middle-class women and white men may have narrowed, this did not carry over to women of colour and poor women. Equality was elusive for those that did not reflect the mainstream. This new movement sought to challenge the prejudices that often underscored earlier feminists.

The term 'intersectionality' was coined by the lawyer Kimberlé Crenshaw 'to describe how race, class, gender, and other individual characteristics 'intersect' with one another and overlap.' The emphasis was on 'layers of oppression' that the black feminist thinker bell hooks (she chose to spell her name using lowercase letters to shift the attention from her identity to her ideas.) argued were ignored and dismissed by her white counterparts.

In other words, many women were disadvantaged not only because they were women but also because of race, poverty and religion, for example. These stories were untold, with 'white' feminists crowding the activism space and securing solutions for their middle-class suburban problems.

Third-wave feminists also challenged the idea of 'heteronormativity', that only heterosexual relationships were valid and sought to be allies with LGBTQ groups. Intersectionality thus meant that these marginalised groupings had to unite against their collective oppression and help each other to bring about change. Many Muslim women, especially those studying at Western universities, are attracted to intersectional feminism. They can easily place their sense of genuine injustices they faced within their communities, many of which had moved away from Islamic principles and the Islamophobia they feel in western societies.

Connecting with other women who face prejudice enables them to find acceptability from some members of broader society, a human impulse everyone craves. This was particularly important after 9/11 when thugs from politics and the streets used Muslim women to symbolise a religion that needed modernisation. The more disadvantaged you were, the deeper your injustice, and so many feminist groups started to make a common cause with Muslims.

Third-wave feminism sought to explain the world through this prism and blamed injustice on structural problems in society. There may be some truths to the analysis, but this form of feminism sought to define oppression in terms Islam would reject. For a Muslim, justice is premised upon Islamic terms. A woman who is refused education is subject to domestic violence and denied inheritance rights is facing injustice. Those such as LGBTQI+ activists that seek to spread fahisha (immorality) by challenging heterosexuality as the norm cannot be seen as seeking justice. For it to be valid, social and political activism must be rooted in Islam.

Fourth Wave Feminism
It is characterised as queer, sex-positive, trans-inclusive, pro-reproductive rights, body-positive, and digitally driven. It seeks to deconstruct gender norms further and asks the question, who are women? This form

of progressive feminism sought to challenge the assumptions of past feminists, some 'cancelling' icons of the feminist movement like Germaine Greer. Fourth-wave activism has included The 'Me Too' movement, 'Slut Walks', 'Free The Nipple' and 'The Women's March.'

When we look at the 'women's rights' that feminists today are advocating for, we can see some overlaps with Islam. The frame work of these rights are defined by Allah and his messenger (saw). Here are a few:

- The right to vote.
- The right to education.
- The right to own property and inherit wealth.
- The right to choose who you marry as long as they are Muslim.
- Sexual assault and domestic violence against women must end.

But many other rights go entirely against Shariah and if a Muslim were to act upon them it would lead them to jahanum:

- The right to be a lesbian, bisexual or change gender, i.e. non-binary or transgender.

- The right to love and marry a non-Muslim.

- Abortion on demand at any time without any reason, as it's a woman's choice what she does with her body.

- The right to use her sexuality for profit so immodest modelling, prostitution, pornography and sexualising oneself are ok.

- The right to not follow an Islamic rule if it is not 'equally applied to men' i,e. women should lead salah in mixed congregations; fathers should not be the head of the house.

In the name of egalitarianism, Muslim feminist thinkers such as Amina Wadud, Asma Barlas and Ziba Mir-Hosseini support these unislamic opinions.

Feminists are hypocrites when it comes to Muslim women's rights. Let me explain. Why are vocal feminists such as Meghan Markle, Mindy Kaling, Zendaya, Priyanka Chopra and Oprah Winfrey silent about Muslim women's right to practice their faith in occupied Palestine, Kashmir or East Turkestan? Why are no global feminist marches organised to show outrage against the hijab bans in France and India? Historically feminists have supported colonialism and more recently the US invasion of Iraq and Afghanistan. They only support Muslim women when it suits them or if we are disobeying Allah.

Inshallah, after reading this chapter, I hope you have a clearer idea about what feminism is and how you have to question what feminists are saying because their beliefs and goals are very different to ours. If you want to continue learning about feminism, enrol in the Islam and feminism course on my website www.smartmuslima.com.

YOUR MUSLIM FAMILY

A family is a blessing: hugs, homemade meals, and companionship. You feel safe, loved and cherished when you're with your family. Islamic history and practice value the family as the beating heart of a community. When constructed correctly, the family provides companionship in an increasingly individualist world. Families are key to the well-being of all its members, young and old, and provide an economic safety net that distributes wealth through obligations and rights.

Did you know that the Islamic family is one of the most important factors that attract non-Muslims from liberal society, especially women, to Islam? The definition of family in the West may have strayed from its religious roots, but this is not the case with us. Our sacred text and prophetic tradition define what family means to us.

Muslim families begin with a husband and wife. Love, romance and intimacy have all been given a unique private place by Allah in the beautiful institution of marriage. Ibn Abbas reported: The Messenger of Allah (saw) said: *'We do not see for those who love one another anything like marriage.' (Sunan Ibn Majah)*

I know marriage is not on the horizon for you now, but it's a good idea to understand it from an Islamic lens earlier rather than later. So, what purpose does Islam give to marriage? Allah made the overarching aim of marriage to achieve tranquillity and contentment in the union. He says, *'It is He who created you all from one soul, and from it made its mate so that he might find comfort in her' (Al-Araf, 7:189).*

This union is meant to be an intimate relationship, and through its companionship comes comfort. He said, *'Another of His signs is that He created spouses from among yourselves for you to live with, in tranquillity: He ordained love and kindness between you. There truly are signs in this for those who reflect.' (Ar-Rum, 30:21)*. Tranquillity does not merely come through a nikah contract. Rather it comes through a conscious and sustained effort from both husband and wife to live as companions and create peacefulness in the home.

Islam laid out the objectives of married life, and the shari'ah laid out the rights and obligations of both husband and wife. *'Wives have [rights] similar to their [obligations], according to what is recognised to be fair, and husbands have a degree [of right] over them: [both should remember that] God is almighty and wise' (Al-Baqarah,2:228)*. The Sahabah understood 'rights similar' to mean the wife deserved the same compassion and kindness as the husband. This is why Ibn' Abbas said,

'Indeed, I spruce myself up for my wife, and she adorns herself for me, and I love that I should redeem all the rights I have over my wife so that she should redeem all the rights she has over me, because Allah (swt) said, 'Wives have [rights] similar to their [obligations], according to what is recognised to be fair.'[33]

Allah has ordered that spouses should love and respect each other. Men, who are generally physically stronger than women, should be mindful of this natural imbalance. The Qur'an implores men to *'Live with them in accordance with what is fair and kind' (An-Nisa, 4:19)*.

Companionship is more than just paying for the household expenses or managing the home, although these are essential obligations. It is a higher objective that comes through intimacy and work. Needless to say, the Messenger (saw) stressed the importance to men, even if they possessed the most 'macho' of qualities, to consciously reframe their relationship with their wives, *'The best amongst you is the one who is best to his wives, and I am the best of you to my wives.' Reported by al-Haakim and Ibn Hibbaan on the authority of Aisha (ra)*

Man as a caretaker

Islam places the man in the position of 'qawwam', or caretakers, *'Men are the caretakers of women, as men have been provisioned by Allah over women and tasked with supporting them financially.' (An-Nisa, 4:39)* To be a caretaker or qawwam is not a statement of superiority nor a license to subject women to injustice because the Qur'an states, *'Treat them fairly. If you happen to dislike them, you may hate something which Allah turns into a great blessing' (An-Nisa,4:19).*

This position Islam has given to men is a duty to look after women, not to allow their mothers, wives, daughters, sisters, aunties etc. to become destitute and to protect them from those that wish to cause them harm. This places the responsibility upon the father and husband to take their duties seriously, whether through work or other means to provide security or finances to enable the family members to flourish. The obligation of providing has been uniquely given to the husband and not the wife.

Liberals arrogantly criticise this to be an attitude of an old-fashioned bygone era. But let's be honest, do we really care what they think? Their beliefs and morals are utterly different to ours, and when we look at their divorce rates, it shows they are in no position to lecture us about marriage or family. Allah, in His wisdom, recognises the fundamental differ-

98

ences between men and women. On average, men are physically stronger than women and so have been blessed with this caretaking duty.

In a world of so-called equality, women find themselves in a position where they are equally accountable for the upkeep of the family. This capitalist trap, which the entire world has now become a prisoner of, places the incredible work of bringing up children and managing the household as a demeaning activity. This does not mean that, according to the shari'ah, a woman cannot earn, nor is it a license to favour men in education over women. Islam obliged both genders to gain knowledge, whether Islamic or worldly – but instead, Islam set differing primary duties for men and women. And through collective efforts, Islam created a balance to make the family unit work in harmony.

The responsibilities of a husband are different from that of a wife. A husband is obliged to strive and provide, and the wife is tasked with the primary responsibility of bringing up the children and managing the household. These, of course, are not exclusive tasks, the dynamics of marital life will mean both the husband and wife would support each other in their duties, as the Messenger (saw) showed us, but the duty remains for both men and women.

Allah says, *'Women have rights similar to those of men equitably, although men have a degree of responsibility above them. And Allah is Almighty, All-Wise.' (Al-Baqarah, 2:228)*. This illustrates this balance Islam sought to create. The meaning of a man's 'responsibility above them' is to provide and protect. It is worth briefly noting that many men have responded negatively to feminism by depicting Islam as a religion calling for male superiority.

By doing this, they echo the broader culture wars in western society, where conservatives rail against progressives and look to return to another form of jahiliyyah (ignorance), where women were denied the most basic rights. We have to transcend the divisive politics of the West.

Feminists accuse Islam of being patriarchal

Most young women that loosely describe themselves as 'feminists' don't realise how too many feminists, the programme of unravelling the family is a central plank of their project. This is because the family represents and embeds what they call a patriarchal society. It reinforces the position of the husband and father as the head of the household and subjects women to a culture of domesticity and free labour, all of which holds women back. It is incorrectly assumed that liberal feminism is about choice. But if women choose to play the role, even if it is not exclusively, as an empathetic mother, partner, and manager of the household, she is somehow demeaning herself to men and upholding patriarchy.

Smash the patriarchy

I'm sure you have heard the slogan 'Smash the patriarchy!' But do you know what it means? Feminists use the idea of 'patriarchy' to depict the unequal power relationship between men and women. The word means 'rule by the father'. Some feminists use patriarchy to describe the structure of the family and the dominance of the father and husband within it. Early Liberal feminists used patriarchy to draw attention to society's unequal distribution of rights.

Therefore, the face of patriarchy they highlight is the underrepresentation of women in senior positions in business, politics and public life. This limited rejection of patriarchy, a public-facing one, was challenged by the new waves of feminism that arose in the 1960s. They argued that the patriarchal family lies at the heart of a systematic, institutionalised process of male supremacy and female subordination in all walks of life. According to them, female oppression originates in the family, so the aim of their activism focused on traditional family structures such as the one advocated by Islam.

In her famous 1975 interview in The Saturday Review, Simone de Beauvoir argued, 'No woman should be authorised to stay at home to raise her children. Society should be different. Women should not have that choice, precisely because if there is such a choice, too many women will make that one... In my opinion, as long as the family and the myth of the family and the myth of maternity and the maternal instinct are not destroyed, women will still be oppressed.'

Gender is a social construct

De Beauvoir, who wrote *The Second Sex* and is a revered figure in the feminist movement, echoed what had now become an article of faith in feminist circles that women and men were the same in their biological and psychological makeup. One could not, therefore, accept that women were 'prisoners of biology' and that reproduction made them more maternal and empathetic. This meant that women and men were androgynous, gender merely a social construct that did not lend itself to any particular social role. 'A woman is not born, but rather becomes,' that is, society designates for her the role of 'woman', relegating her to what De Beauvoir called 'the second sex'.

Women were therefore brainwashed to play the role of a mother, and it was a duty to free her of these responsibilities. This socialisation process had to be challenged to smash the patriarchy. Of course, not all feminists believed that the family needed to be uprooted entirely; although many radical feminists advocated for this and the sexual revolution aided their cause, the family nonetheless was an institution that needed to be reimagined with a more modern take.

Betty Friedan had the most significant impact on second-wave feminism and reassessments of the family. Her provocative book, *The Feminine Mystique*, reflected her personal journey and her own dissatisfaction with American suburban living. She spoke of the monotony of her existence and that of many women in her position who felt restrained by household duties that revolved around motherhood and interior decor. This 'comfortable concentration camp' meant women could only aspire to second-class status at best.

Kate Millet expanded on patriarchy as a system of repression in her book *Sexual Politics (1970)*, arguing that it could be found in all walks of life, in law, government, literature, popular culture, and more generally, college and the family. This system of patriarchy started in the home, where the father was the head of the household and began the process of socialisation into male and female roles. Patriarchy's 'chief institution' is the family. It is both a mirror of and a connection with the larger society, a patriarchal unit within a patriarchal whole. To undo the web of patriarchy, one had to start with undoing the traditional family.

The thoughts of second-wave feminism had an impact, probably most notably upon popular culture. It is arguably within popular culture that progressives have successfully sought to fight the patriarchy. Films, TV shows and novels reinforce this dislike of the traditional family and challenge this socialisation process. The father is most often subject to the wrath of mainstream productions.

Disrespecting dads

On the one hand, you have the idiot dad who has been a television stereotype for as long as I can remember; examples include Homer Simpson and Ted Wheeler from *Stranger Things*. And you also have overbearing fathers who bully their kids, i.e. Peter Griffin from *Family Guy* and the violent Pakistani dad in the movie *Hala*. When they become a constant, these images leave an indelible effect on the minds of teenagers: fathers should be subject to ridicule and the focus of their liberation. On the flip side, a good father, such as the one in the movie *Blockers*, facilitates his daughter losing her virginity on prom night. This depiction is far from accidental; popular culture reflects the dominant ideological character of society.

The attack against the family has also extended to the Muslim family. A tsunami of stories, some real, some imagined, depict the Muslim family to be a regressive institution. Honour killings, misogyny and forced marriages are terms that have become synonymous with Islam. I will not paper over the challenges the Muslim family faces in a world of globalisation and in the absence of proper Islamic governance that aims to secure justice for all. However, the ordinary lives of two billion people are reduced to the worst excesses of the Taliban or those men who, in Muslim countries, subject women to violence because of a lack of systems of accountability. Most Muslim families have been remarkably resilient to these liberalising forces. Alhamdulilah, Muslim family life remains at the heart of our community experiences.

What is the Muslim family, and how does Islam view patriarchy?

The first thing to say is that terms like 'patriarchy' have been employed in a social and cultural context laden with layers of meaning. It comes from a language of liberalism, a response to the perceived imbalances of power in a society. Muslims should not be beholden to these terms, whether as a means to explain overlaps with Islam or as a means to apologise and find hadith or even Qur'anic verses to justify an argument that Islam is against patriarchy. Too many Muslims attempt to confirm or critique debates with a uniquely western foundation.

Second-wave feminism was responding to the suburban American family and the problems women faced within it. Islam stands alone as a system of thought that can be directly accredited to divine revelation. It is worth reminding you and myself that, *'When God and His Messenger have decided on a matter that concerns them, it is not fitting for any believing man or woman to claim freedom of choice in that matter: whoever disobeys God and His Messenger is far astray' (Al-Ahzab, 33:36)*

Thus, the believer, whether influenced by liberal feminism or conservatism, must surrender to Islam and approach the revelation without preconceived world views. These ideological frameworks harm our submission to Allah. In summary, we cannot use these broad, ideologically loaded terms like 'patriarchy' to define Islam's position. It does an injustice to Islam to do so. At the same time, we cannot negate well-established Islamic rules to find a way to conform to modernity.

Obedience

Feminists hate the word 'obedience'. It reeks of patriarchy when religion tells a wife to obey her husband. Interestingly they don't have a problem with women' obeying' their male bosses' or a female soldier following her sergeant's commands. Many young women (and men) who are a product of a culture that looks to uproot the family and smash the patriarchy are also uncomfortable with the word obedience. But it is undeniable that the overwhelming narrations both from the Qur'an and hadith place as one of the rights of a husband that the wife obeys him. Feminists point to this imbalance in the family to confirm what Kate Millet claimed to be the patriarchal family that needs to be destroyed.

This has led some who call themselves 'Muslim feminists' to look to reinterpret Islam to be in line with a post-patriarchal reading. I.e. Asma Barlas, Amina Wadud, and Musawah.org. These feminists want to approach the text from a liberal lens and 'cleanse' the shari'ah. I am not going to question their sincerity; indeed, many are responding to the abuse of terms such as obedience to subject women to unspeakable repression and violence within the household. But the fact is that their remedies contribute to destroying the natural balance Islam sets in the family and undermines tranquillity within the home.

So let's have a frank discussion about 'obedience'. As I have already said, men have been described as 'qawwam' – caretakers. They are the amir (leader) over the family; the Messenger (saw) said, *'All of you are shepherds, and every one of you is responsible for his herd... a man is the shepherd over his family, and a woman is a shepherd over her husband's house and children' (Al-Bukhari and Muslim).* This hadith clearly gives the role of leadership to the husband. This does not mean he should conduct his tasks by dominating and dictating, as this would destroy the harmony in the household. The wife should be consulted. Allah (swt) describes those that respond to their Lord as those that *'conduct their affairs by mutual consultation' (Ash-Shura, 42:38)*.

The subject of this verse was the Messenger (saw), who has the foremost right to be obeyed after Allah, yet his Lord requested that he consult the sahabah and Muslims in their affairs. A pertinent example to illustrate this is, at a critical moment after the signing of the Treaty of Hudaybiyyah, the Messenger (saw) consulted his wife, Umm Salama, on how to deal with his companions that were unhappy with the terms of the agreement. Umm Salama showed political insight when she told him how he should manage the situation. We know from the science of fiqh (usul al-fiqh) that when a command is given to the Messenger by Allah (saw) in the Qur'an, it is a command for all of us.

Simply put, no one in a position of authority should neglect the wisdom and blessings that come from consultation (shura). It improves the decision and strengthens the union. The husband thus makes all the major decisions in the household after considering the opinions of its members and should be willing to show flexibility.

To obey does not mean that a wife's role in a marriage is to be a passive bystander. She has the right, from the sunnah, to debate with her husband and criticise what he says. This is because she is a companion and not a servant. In his home, the Messenger of Allah (saw) was a companion to his wives, not an oppressive ruler over them, despite being the leader of a state and despite his role as a Prophet and Messenger. 'Umar bin al-Khattab reflected on this in a very long but pertinent narration,

'By Allah, in the pre-Islamic period of ignorance, we did not pay atten-tion to women until Allah revealed regarding them what He revealed re-garding them and assigned for them what He has assigned. Once while I was thinking over a certain matter, my wife said, 'I recommend that you do so-and-so.' I said to her, 'What have you got to do with this the is mat-ter? Why do you poke your nose in a matter which I want to see fulfilled?' She said, how strange you are, O son of Al-Khattab! You don't want to be argued with, whereas your daughter, Hafsa surely, argues with Allah's Messenger (saw) so much that he remains angry for a full day!'

`Umar then reported; how he at once put on his outer garment and went to Hafsa and said to her, 'O my daughter! Do you argue with Allah's Messenger (saw) so that he remains angry the whole day?' Hafsa said, 'By Allah, we argue with him....' Umar added, 'Then I went out to Umm Salama's house, who was one of my relatives, and I talked to her. She said, 'O son of Al-Khattab! It is rather astonishing that you interfere in everything; you even want to interfere between Allah's Apostle and his wives!' (He then thought), by Allah, by her talk, she influenced me so much that I lost some of my anger. I left her (and went home).' (Bukhari)

This hadith informs us about the standard given to us by the best of cre-ation and the mother of the believers. A wife has a right to question and give her input in the decisions of daily life, and the husband is responsi-ble for accepting her advice. In the end, however, the decision rests with him as the amir over the household, and she has to accept this because this is the role Allah has given him. In the same way, in any workplace, a manager would make a decision, and it would have to be accepted by the workers under them. The difference here is that a family is not a workplace, and the husband has an equal responsibility to support his wife lovingly and compassionately.

The limits of obedience

In shari'ah, total obedience is only to Allah (swt), the Messenger (saw), and his established sunnah. Beyond submission to Islam, all other forms of obedience must be qualified. A well-known hadith states, *'There is no obedience to anyone if it is disobedience to Allah. Verily, obedience is only in good conduct.' (Bukhari).*

This lays out the clear principle that Muslims cannot obey anyone who asks them to commit disobedience to Allah, even if that's their parents or husband. After this clear-cut injunction, obedience to any human being is based on the rights and obligations owed to them. A caliph (leader of all Muslims) should be obeyed, but this is only when it comes to the obligations Islam has established the citizenry owes to the caliph. If the leader commanded Muslims to divorce their spouses, then obedience here would have no value, as this is beyond the jurisdiction of a leader.

Similarly, the father's obedience over a child is qualified by what is within his rights. A father, for example, cannot dictate whom the child marries and what employment they should seek, as this is beyond their right. Scholars argue when a father requests from his child a matter that is beyond his right, then to obey is not an obligation but rather a mandub, a recommendation that earns him reward but not punishment. Likewise, a husband cannot tell his wife to spend her money in a way he deems fit or dictates how she uses her property or forces her to change her madhab (school of thought). Rather in the areas of his responsibility, after consultation, the final decision rests with him, as he is the amir of the household. After this, the wife is responsible for following that decision. For example, deciding where their children should go to school or moving to a new city after consultation is the right of the husband to make.

Liberal feminists detest the language of obedience, even with the above caveats and qualifications. They see marriage as premised on equality, which is unobtainable and leads to marital disharmony. A Muslim confidently knows what Allah informed us, *'We created man—We know what his soul whispers to him: We are closer to him than his jugular vein—' (Qaf, 50:16).* Allah has given us a system of living that organises our lives. The perfect way in which He designed marriage to be a companionship that aims for tranquillity, a union where both men and women find comfort, a place where children are loved and nurtured and where their characters are built. It is a garden within which upright personalities are cultivated.

Therefore, the role of a mother is central to the Islamic family, as she is responsible for the nurture and education of the children. This is reflected in the hadith where someone asked the Prophet (saw), *'Who is most deserving of good care for me?' The Prophet replied, 'Your mother.' Then the man asked and who after that? He repeated, 'Your mother.' The man asked, 'And who after that?' the Prophet repeated, 'Your mother and then your father, then your nearest relatives in order of closeness.' (Bukhari)*

In another narration, the role of the Muslim family is beautifully illustrated. A man once came to 'Umar ibn Al-Khattaab, the second Caliph of Islam, complaining of his sons' disobedience to him. 'Umar summoned the boy and spoke of his disobedience to his father and his neglect of his rights. The boy replied: 'O Ameer al-Mu'mineen (Prince of believers)!

Hasn't a child rights over his father?' 'Certainly', replied 'Umar. 'What are they, Ameer al-Mu'mineen?' 'That he should choose his mother, give him a good name and teach him the Book (the Quran).' 'O Ameer al-Mu'mineen! My father did nothing of this. My mother was a Magian (fire worshipper). He gave me the name of Julalaan (meaning dung beetle or scarab), and he did not teach me a single letter of the Quran.' Turning to the father, Umar (may Allah be pleased with him) said: 'You have come to me to complain about the disobedience of your son. You have failed in your duty to him before he has failed in his duty to you; you have done wrong to him before he has wronged you.'

When it goes wrong?

Liberal feminists would have us believe that modernity, loosely defined as a world defined by the ideas that came out of Europe in the seventeenth and eighteenth centuries, are universal standards. They utilise terms like the 'dark ages' and 'medieval' to connote a bleak period before the advent of liberalism. Islamic history is often characterised as part of this period simply because most western commentators lazily lump all religions into a single form. Behind this simplistic view of the world is the belief in liberal progress.

When European society dispensed with religion, it decided that humans could determine right and wrong based on their ability to reason. An external creator was not required to make sense of the world; instead, as humans progressed, they would come to a better way. The 'traditional' family was a relic of the past. Talking about the primary roles of men and women undermines the progress human society has come to. When liberal feminists view Islamic family structure, they project their own experiences with their religions and what they believe is progress and conclude that Islam needs to reform.

But this requirement to 'change with the times' would not have any currency if families within our communities lived up to the Islamic standard. When we look at the state of (some, not all) Muslim families, they are not glowing adverts for family bliss. Stories related by exhausted wives are filled with too much detail to be invented or ignored. Scarred mothers tell their daughters to 'learn from my mistakes, get an education and career, so you don't have to rely on a man.' To make matters worse, religion is used to justify the mistreatment, for example, denying girls access to education, preferential treatment of sons, forced marriage, and physical abuse. This is one reason Muslim women turn away from Islam and seek validation from feminism. They turn to local and online feminist organisations that take their issues seriously and place those concerns within the context of a larger feminist struggle against patriarchal systems. What is often appealing here is not so much the philosophy of liberal feminism but the promise of change.

I want to address the use of religion to justify attitudes that contradict the prophetic sunnah, for example, denying girls an education. This unislamic attitude comes from a response to the overwhelming social and moral decline we see around us. To 'save' our children, they must be isolated as much as possible from the shameless society, even if that means their rights are withheld. Within time a fiqh is developed that picks the most difficult rules in the hope that this society will not impact our families. This does not help Islam. Islam sent messengers to change society, not to enable society to change the timeless revelation from Allah (swt).

When we see unjust behaviour in our communities, we must speak up. This is a challenging task, and parents, imams, teachers, authors, and scholars must all play a role. We should focus on creating an environment that supports Muslim women and recognises their pivotal importance in our communities. This means there has to be constructive work within the Muslim communities to reassert Islamic practice.

MAKING SENSE OF PUBERTY

P uberty is one strand in the tapestry that is life. You need some framework to put this stage of your life into perspective. The context you can and should understand is how Allah creates babies, and the key role women play in procreation and the continued existence of the human race.

How Allah creates babies

Every baby is created in its mother's womb. It is related by Anas ibn Malik that the Prophet (saw) said, '*Allah the Mighty and Majestic appoints an angel to every womb who says, 'O Lord! A drop! O Lord, A clot! O, Lord! A lump of flesh! 'Then, if He desires to complete His creation, He does so, and the angel asks, 'Is it to be male or female? Wretched or happy? What is its provision? What is its lifespan?' This is all decreed in the mother's womb.*' (Muslim)

Over nine months, the baby develops from one stage to the other until it reaches full term. Allah says: '*It is He who has created you from dust, then from a drop of seed, then from a clot; Then He brings you forth as a child, then ordains that you reach the age of full strength and afterwards that you become old-though some among you die before- and that you reach an appointed term, in order that you may understand.*' (Ghafir, 40:67)

Understanding the prominent role Allah has given women in reproduction is crucial. Allah chose women to give birth to and nurture babies. He designed our bodies so we can perform this blessed and demanding task. You are born with two ovaries and a uterus. The ovaries contain ova (eggs). Ova are the female gametes or sex cells. The uterus is a muscular bag with a soft lining. It is where a baby develops until its birth. We produce hormones called oestrogen and progesterone, which cause changes in your body during puberty.

Why do girls have periods?

Periods begin when your body is mature enough to have a baby. Every month, the lining of your uterus (womb) gets thicker with tissue, and your ovaries release an egg. If a sperm fertilises the egg, the tissue stays where it is to help with pregnancy. But if the egg isn't fertilised, your body sheds the tissue through the vagina. That tissue is the blood you see, and this monthly process is called menstruation.

For your well being it is vital that you understand your body and the role organs and hormones play as well as the menstrual cycle. You will learn about the female reproductive system in Biology, which is a good thing. Looking at scientific diagrams of the human body is okay to gain knowledge. There is nothing 'shameful or disgusting' about your body; Allah created it. Our bodies are a trust (amanah); the Prophet (saw) said, *'Indeed, your own self has rights over you'* (*Abu Dawud*). How can you take care of your health and hygiene if you do not know your body? A healthy body is a gift from your Creator. Allah instructs you how to take care of it in the Quran and Sunnah - by embracing the halal and leaving the haram.

Alhamdulillah, you will experience many exciting stages in your life. Allah placed you into this world as a pure, innocent baby, and with every passing year, you will increase in strength and transform from a young girl to a young woman. Puberty and beginning your period is one stage in your life. Aisha (ra) narrated that the Prophet (saw) said, *'This is something that Allah has decreed for the daughters of Adam.' (Sunan An-Nasai. Chapter 1, The Book of Purification).* Your body will change and mature, so it will be ready to be a mother when you marry. Inshallah, over time, and with the help of Allah, you will learn to carry yourself as a confident Muslim woman.

When Does Puberty Begin?

Puberty can start at different ages. Islamically puberty cannot begin for a girl before the age of nine. You've reached puberty if you haven't started menstruating by fifteen (in Islamic years). A girl's first period usually begins between nine and sixteen. The typical age is twelve and a half years. Vaginal discharge that is either white or yellowish will start to appear before your period starts. If you want to keep your underwear clean, you might want to consider using panty liners.

Around 6 to 18 months following the beginning of discharge, your menstruation can begin. First, menstruations are often light. You'll get your period about once a month and lose a small amount of blood through your vagina for two to eight days. A period doesn't mean you'll bleed all day. It's normal to stop bleeding for a few hours and then bleed a bit more. The amount of blood you lose during your period is about 30-70 ml. When your period is at its heaviest, the blood will be red. On lighter days, it may be pink, brown or black.

You will need to wear a pad in your underwear to collect the blood. Sometimes periods aren't regular, especially when they first start, and it might be challenging to plan exactly when you'll get your period. Everyone begins puberty at different times. It's entirely natural to start before or after your friends or cousins. Speak to your mum or a female relative you trust if you're concerned about puberty starting earlier or later. Inshallah, you can also visit a female doctor with them if you are anxious. You have nothing to worry about as long as you eat healthily and get plenty of sleep. It is a special time chosen by Allah and will occur when your body is ready for it.

Alhamdullilah, once you start your period, you are no longer a child. You are now accountable to Allah for all your words and actions. So it's important that you learn the rules about your obligations, such as salah, fasting, cleanliness, hijab etc. and practice them in your daily routine.

Your period

I am sure you will have many questions about the details of fiqh rules surrounding the issue of periods, ghusl etc., which, unfortunately, I cannot answer in the short space of this chapter. However, you can get answers from knowledgeable people who have studied this subject. Ask your mum or another female relative to help you find the answers, depending on which madhab (school of Islamic thought your family follows), i.e. Hanafi, Shafi, Malaki.

Here is a summary of the issues you need to know once your period begins. Sometimes you can start your period when you're not expecting to, so it's always a good idea to be prepared.

- Keep a change of underwear and sanitary pads in your bag in case you start your period when you are out.Ask an adult like your parent, carer or school nurse about things to help with pain or discomfort, like hot water bottles or pain relief tablets. Gentle exercise can help relieve pain and bloating - try stretching or walking.

- Write down when your period begins and ends to track what's normal for you so you can notice any changes, as periods can be irregular when they first start; many Islamic rules depend on this.

- Muslims are required to take care of their personal hygiene by assuring that they are well-groomed, and their bodies, clothes, and surroundings are clean. Our beloved Prophet Muhammad (saw) said about the importance of purification that: *'Cleanliness is half the faith (Iman).' (Sahih Muslim)*. So for hygiene reasons, wrap your used pad and throw it in the bin. Don't flush down the toilet. If your underwear has blood on it, wash it as soon as possible. Be considerate towards your family members. No one wants to see blood-stained pads or underwear lying in the bathroom.

- During your period, you do not have to pray salah. The Prophet (saw) said, *'... a woman can neither pray nor fast during her menses' (Muslim)*. You don't have to make up your salah. This is a blessing from Allah. Do not cut all connection with Allah. Make wudu, sit and make dhikr, duas, read durood etc., so you keep the routine of praying. Tell your parents when you are on your period so you can have a lie in and they don't wake you up for fajr!

- You will need to make up the missed fasts after Ramadan. Aishah said: *'When we would have our menses during the lifetime of the Prophet, we were ordered to make up the days of fasting that we had missed but were not ordered to make up the prayers that we had* missed.' *(Bukhari)*. Some girls pretend they are fasting because they are too embarrassed to tell their parents they are on their period. That is so ridiculous; please don't do that. You are making life harder for yourself. Just tell your mum, and she can tell your dad.

• Once your period bleeding has finished, it's fard (obligatory) to make ghusl. Ghusl is the full-body ritual purification. It is compulsory before performing various rituals and prayers for any adult Muslim after sexual intercourse/ejaculation or completion of the menstrual cycle. Women used to send A'isha little boxes containing pieces of cotton cloth still showing some yellowness. 'A'isha would say, *'Do not rush [to do ghusl] until you see white cotton,' meaning by that purity from menstruation.' (Bukhari)* After you are sure that all discharge has changed to white, you are ready to make ghusl and begin praying again.

How to do ghusl

This is a general outline; please find out the exact details depending on the madhab your family follows.

1. Make the niyyah (intention) to perform ghusl for purification.
2. Wash your private parts thoroughly with water.
3. Perform wudu (ablution) except for washing your feet, which you can do later after bathing the body. Sniff water up your nose to the point where bone goes from soft to hard. Gargle three times.
4. Starting with your head, wash the entire body, first the right side, then the left. Use a scented body wash as the female companions used perfumed pieces of cloth to wipe off menstrual blood and clean their private parts three times. (Bukhari).

5. Wash the body three times, rubbing your body. The minimum is once. Make sure your clean your belly button and behind ear-rings and rings. Every inch of the body must be wet.

6. Once you have completed the ghusl, recite the dua: 'O Allah, make me of those who return to You often in repentance and make me of those who remain clean and pure.'[34]

During puberty, you will undergo several changes at a fast rate because of the hormones produced in your body. Some changes may be more ob-vious than others. It can take up to four years for all of the changes to take effect, but it can happen sooner.

What to expect

Puberty is a normal part of growing up and can impact you in different ways. It can be stressful not knowing what to expect, especially when people might say different things about what happens during puberty. But don't worry. Inshallah, you can find all the answers you need right here. Let's go through the changes you'll experience during puberty.

Spots and acne are common

It's normal to get spots and blackheads during puberty, and you might have acne. Spots and acne are caused by hormones, not by being dirty or not washing. Your hormones may also cause you to sweat more. This is because your sweat glands change and produce more sweat to help con-trol your body's temperature. Keeping the areas that you sweat, like your armpits, groin, and private parts, clean and dry will help to stop any smell from developing. It's important to wash once a day, wear clean un-derwear and clothes, and wear deodorant. If you have long hair and you may find your scalp becomes sweaty at night. So remember to massage your scalp and wash your hair regularly.

What exactly is acne, and what can I do about it?

Acne is a skin condition that looks like spots and blackheads, often on your face and back. Avoid squeezing or picking at your spots, and always remove any makeup before going to bed. It is challenging to live with, and you might feel embarrassed or depressed because of your acne, and unfortunately, other teenagers will make fun of you. I had severe acne as a teenager, and I hated it. Not looking in the mirror too much helps! Out of sight out of mind. Remember, it won't last forever and talking about your feelings with someone you trust can help.

Acne may not affect you, but if it does, there are gels and lotions available to treat it, or your doctor may prescribe medication. It's a good idea to keep yourself clean and healthy by washing. Over washing can worsen acne by drying your skin, so avoid washing the affected region more than twice a day.

You will grow body hair and pubic hair.

Puberty causes hair to grow under your arms, on your private parts (pubic hair) and your legs. Your facial hair can also become thicker. Most people develop pubic and body hair; however, some have more hair than others. The Prophet (saw) instructed both genders to shave or trim the pubic hair (around the private areas till the pubic hairline) and hair of the underarms within a period of forty days. *Anas (ra) narrates that Rasulullah (saw) stipulated the time for trimming the moustache, clipping the nails, plucking the armpit hair, and shaving the private parts, that it should not exceed forty days. (Sahih Muslim)*

'The fitrah is five things – or five things are part of the fitrah – circumcision, shaving the pubes, cutting the nails, plucking the armpit hairs, and trimming the moustache.' (Al-Bukhari & Muslim)

Some girls say, 'No one has the right to tell us what to do with our bodies and that following the sunnah to remove pubic hair represents the most basic rules of the patriarchy (I explain what this means in the feminism chapter). You are being trained by men to hide the fact that you have gone through puberty, and being considered feminine is about remaining a girl – not being too hairy.'

This argument makes no sense as Islamically; men are also told to remove their pubic hair. No one is attempting to police young women's bodies. Both genders follow the Messenger of Allah (saw) as Allah Most High says, *'If you obey him, you will be guided.' (An-Nur, 24:54).*

How do I remove my pubic hair?
Removing your pubic hair is uncomfortable and tricky. Please speak to your mum or sister for advice before you do it the first time. I know it is an embarrassing subject to bring up, but you don't want to harm yourself, and they will be happy to advise you.

Should you remove the hair on your face, arms and legs?
Most images of women you will see online are 'hairless'. Smooth and silky.This establishes a fake vision of what it means to be beautiful and puts pressure on you to dislike your body hair. It's not just about the pressure to be girlish. Being a hair-free female is also a pretty white standard of beauty.

121

Islam does not require you to remove all the hair from your arms, legs and face, but you may if you like. Your feelings regarding body hair will alter before you get married, and if you have thick hair on your arms and legs, you probably will want to remove it. There is nothing wrong with wanting to appear attractive. Having a hairy top lip or overgrown brows might make you self-conscious. It's okay to remove upper lip hair, but don't turn it into an obsession.

Speak to a knowledgeable person regarding what forms of hair removal techniques are permitted in Islam before you begin treatment. For example, laser treatment is very popular. However, you are not allowed to show your awrah or private parts to another woman for the sake of laser hair removal. Many young women don't know that. We don't choose a haram method to do something halal.

How to remove your pubic hair

There are different ways to remove your hair. You could use a razor with shaving gel, cream, or an electric razor. To avoid shaving rash, it's a good idea to wash before shaving, keep your razor clean and replace the blades or your disposable razor when the edges are blunt. Some women prefer to use hair removal products, like gels or wax, to remove their body hair or use products that make dark facial body hair lighter in colour. If you do, always follow the instructions on the packet and do a patch test on a small skin area first to check for any reactions. You can check with an adult the first time you use a product or if you have any questions. Shaving, waxing or using an electric razor or scissors are ways to remove or trim pubic hair, but other products aren't safe to use close to your vagina.

You will grow taller, your breasts and hips will become bigger

A major change that happens during puberty is that you develop breasts. You hips widen, and so your body will have more curves. Everyone's body develops at different speeds, so try not to compare yourself to others. The size and shape of your breasts, stomach and hips will continue changing throughout your life. Many factors can influence their size and shape, including a healthy diet, exercise, illness, pregnancy, and breastfeeding. Because Allah made us all with distinct physical sizes, our body shapes will also be diverse. There is no standard size or form for breasts and hips.

Changes to your breasts

Breasts come in all shapes and sizes, and they're all normal.

- Having one breast which is bigger than the other is normal.

- It's normal for breasts to feel sore or tender sometimes. This usually happens just before or during your period.
- Breasts can feel heavier or softer before a period

- Nipples come in different shapes and sizes. They can be outwards or inwards. The area around the nipple is called the areola, and it's normal to be a few shades darker than your breast. Sometimes nipples have bumps, pimples or hairs.

- Speak to your mum if you often feel sharp pains or an ache in your breast and if you notice a lump on your breast or anything that doesn't seem usual. She can make an appointment to see a female doctor. Check your breasts for lumps regularly; there is nothing shameful about it.

As your breasts begin to grow, you need to start wearing a bra. This will help you have good posture and prevent shoulder and back pain. It's important to get fitted for a bra in a store to ensure you are wearing the right size, and a sports bra can give more support when exercising. Your mum or another female relative can help you do this.

Observing your body transform should not be a depressing experience. Allah says, *'Indeed, We created humans in the best form.' (At-Tin, 95:4).* So, Allah does not want you to feel bad about your body. Puberty is when you develop from a child to an adult. And that is a good thing. It is a stage in your life that is a blessing. You will feel self-conscious about your curves or lack of curves but be kind to yourself, just as Allah is kind to you. Abu Hurayrah reported that the Prophet ﷺ said: *'Allah does not look at your bodies or at your forms; rather, He looks at your hearts and deeds.' (Sahih Muslim)*

So what makes you feel bad about your body?
Unfortunately, it's wider society and other people. You have to be smart and realise that many of the images of women you see on TikTok, Instagram and Netflix are not natural. People can make their bodies look attractive in the following ways:

- Plastic surgery enhances the size of their breasts and reduces their waist size.

- Filters on the photos can change a person's body shape, making them look thinner or curvy.

- Women wear push-up bras, tummy-flattening underwear and bottom-shaping underwear.

- Marketers use older models when advertising clothes to teenagers. So your body will never look like theirs because you are not as physically developed. They also do this in movies; older actresses in their twenties play 16-year-old high schoolers.

Unfortunately, there is a lot of immodesty and nudity, especially online, so it's hard not to compare yourself to others. Sex sells, and young women quickly learn that flaunting their curves online gets more likes and followers. So they use their 'assets' to market themselves, become famous and get rich. Kylie Jenner, The Kardashians, Lizzo and Bella Hadid are experts at sexual objectification.

Their brand is envy. They want teenagers like you to think, 'I wish I looked like that.' And then they market all the products they use so you believe you can have their gorgeous body. How manipulative and dishonest! They don't care about the harm this causes to your self-esteem and confidence. To feel more positive about your changing body during puberty, do this:

- Know that your value is not measured by how sexy, thin or curvy you are; but by how beautiful you are in the sight of Allah, your Creator. Wanting to look attractive and wearing beautiful clothes is okay if done in a way that does not contradict Islam. *Abdullah ibn Mas'ud (ra) said that the Prophet (saw) said, 'No one will enter Paradise who has an atom's weight of pride in his heart.' A man said, 'What if a man likes his clothes to look good and his shoes to look good?' He said, 'Allah is beautiful and loves beau-*

125

ty. Pride means denying the truth and looking down on people.' (Muslim). Following the prophetic tradition will help you develop a healthy balanced attitude towards your body.

- Relatives will comment on your appearance; try your best to ignore their negative observations. Be polite but don't let them get you down.

- Unfollower people online who make you insecure about your body. Protect your eyes and your mind. Stop looking at semi-naked images of other young women.

- You don't need to copy what other girls are doing online blindly. Why does society expect you to present a sexualised version of yourself for friends or strangers to consume? You are not a product.

- Proudly, wear your hijab and jilbab.

- Eat healthily, limit eating junk food, drink plenty of water, and be active. You will feel better about yourself when you take care of your physical health.

Puberty blockers

I think it's relevant to explain what puberty blockers are. Today, young people are being encouraged to choose their gender-based purely on their subjective feelings rather than the objective reality of their biology. It's called gender self-identification, and it is a modern phenomenon. The name given to this trendy twenty-first-century condition is gender dysphoria. Teenagers are being referred to a hormone specialist to see if they can take hormone blockers as they reach puberty.

Puberty blockers (gonadotrophin-releasing hormone analogues) pause the physical changes of puberty, such as breast development or facial hair. Little is known about the long-term psychological side effects of puberty blockers in children with gender dysphoria.

It's also not known whether hormone blockers affect the development of the teenage brain or children's bones. Side effects may also include hot flushes, fatigue and mood alterations. From the age of 16, teenagers who've been on hormone blockers for at least 12 months may be given cross-sex hormones, also known as gender-affirming hormones.These hormones cause some irreversible changes, such as:

- breast development (caused by taking oestrogen)
- breaking or deepening of the voice (caused by taking testos-terone)

Long-term cross-sex hormone treatment may cause temporary or even permanent infertility. There is some uncertainty about the risks of long-term cross-sex hormone treatment.[35]

It is safe to say that taking puberty blockers is abnormal and goes against the way Allah has created you. They prevent your body from naturally developing the way Allah meant it to and can stop you from having babies. Pharmaceutical companies are using children as guinea pigs; profit is their priority. They are taking advantage of young impressionable girls who feel unhappy with their bodies and offering them puberty blockers to solve their troubles. You need to be smart and not buy into the hype surrounding gender self-identification. Inshallah, read the chapter on to understand this topic thoroughly.

You may experience mood swings

Mood swings are a natural part of puberty. You may feel as if you have no control over your emotions, such as being upbeat one minute and embarrassed or tearful the next. What is causing your mood changes, and what can you do? Hormones, your period, dealing with physical changes, and possibly having acne or body odour can all impact your mood. You may feel self-conscious or have poor self-esteem. It will be beneficial to inform your friends and family that you are experiencing mood swings, so they know you are not purposely being rude to them.

Why is everything suddenly embarrassing?

Embarrassment is an emotion you will experience more often during puberty. It is the uncomfortable feeling you get when you've done something which you think will make you look bad. Feeling embarrassed can be a very upsetting experience. You might feel weird, picked on, stupid, ugly or worthless, even when you've done nothing wrong. You might feel ill, or like you want to cry.

Embarrassment can be a passing feeling that's not a big deal or an overwhelming feeling that's hard to cope with. Sometimes it can seem like the feeling will never go away. It's important to remember that feeling mortified doesn't last forever, and it can get easier to cope with as we understand situations better.

How embarrassment manifests itself

People can feel embarrassed in all kinds of situations. It can be a general feeling, for example, when you meet someone new and find it difficult to talk to them. Sometimes it's a particular thing that makes you feel embarrassed – like saying something which came out wrong or doing something you think other people will laugh at. Other people's behaviour can make you wish you were invisible. Someone's offensive comments about you can make you feel humiliated.

Whatever you're feeling embarrassed about, remember that it's natural to feel this way. Everyone gets embarrassed. And we all do things we feel a bit silly about or something we wish we'd done differently or not at all. It's impossible to be perfect and get things right all the time. Please don't beat yourself up about it. Don't keep replaying the moment; learn to let go.

Situations that can feel embarrassing include:

- Meeting new people. Being scared of 'embarrassing yourself' can often stop you from going out with friends or doing things.
- Feeling uncomfortable about how you look or having low self-esteem.
- Talking about sex or things that happen to your body during puberty.
- Being made to feel embarrassed because of bullying.
- Getting attention for something you've done, like being given an award at school.
- Your family's behaviour or traditions.
- Being made to do things you don't want to or peer pressure to act a certain way.
- Experiencing abuse. Even though abuse is never your fault, some people feel embarrassed to tell someone about it. You're not

alone, don't suffer in silence. Tell an adult family member or friend who can support you.

Try the following strategies next time you feel embarrassed:

Do dua

Turn to Allah for help. If you are facing a stressful situation with other people, make dua in your mind. Ask Allah to help you get out of the situation and have peace of mind.

Make a joke about it

If something isn't that serious, laughing about what went wrong can help you feel better. Laughter can show other people (and yourself) that it isn't something to worry about.

Try to play down or ignore what happened.

Sometimes this can stop you from blushing or feeling really stressed. You might think something was really awkward or humiliating, but other people might not have even noticed. So stay calm. Act like it's no big deal.

Talk to someone you trust

Talking about how you feel can make things seem better or help you understand your feelings. Try talking to a friend or adult who you trust. Alternatively, empty all your feelings onto paper, so you can clear your mind, then tear up the paper and throw it away. Don't think about the embarrassing incident again.

Face up to what you've done

If you feel your behaviour might have upset someone, try to apologise to them. I know it's not easy. You could tell them how sorry you are and you regret what happened. Telling someone can be a first step in moving on. Admitting that you've done something wrong shows you can take responsibility and learn from your mistakes.

You might compare yourself to others

It's very easy to compare yourself to your friends and feel jealous of them, but please remember puberty is a unique journey, and your body will develop at its own pace. It's so easy to look at other girls and wish you had what they had. Jealousy is a sin, and it will cause you nothing but harm. *Abu Huraira reported that the Messenger of Allah (saw) said, 'Save yourself from jealousy. This is because jealousy consumes good deeds just as fire consumes firewood/ grass.' (Sunan Abi Dawud)*. It can very quickly lead to backbiting and making nasty comments about others to make yourself feel better. *Abu Hurairah said: The Messenger of Allah (saw) said, 'Do you know what is backbiting?' The Companions said: 'Allah and His Messenger know better.' Thereupon he said, 'Backbiting is talking about your (Muslim) brother in a manner which he dislikes.' It was said to him: 'What if my (Muslim) brother is as I say.' He said, 'If he is actually as you say, then that is backbiting; but if that is not in him, that is slandering.'*

So think before you speak about other girls, you don't like it when people comment about your looks, so don't act hypocritically. Rather follow the sunnah, *Yazid ibn Asad reported: The Messenger of Allah, (saw), said to me, 'O Yazid, love for people what you love for yourself.' In another nar-*

ration, the Prophet (saw) said, 'Do not treat people but in the way you would love to be treated by them.' (Ahmad)

It's normal for everyone to be different, so putting yourself down won't help.Diversity is part of Allah's plan. In fact, Allah created different skin colours and languages as signs for us to ponder upon. Just as flowers and fruit come in different colours, all are divine signs of Allah's creation; human beings come in different forms. Imagine how dull life would be if we all had the same body shape, nose shape or hair type? *'Among His signs is the creation of the heavens and the earth and the diversity of your languages and your colours. Verily, in that are signs for people of knowledge.' (Ar-Rum, 30:22).* Taqwa is the only quality that makes someone righteous in the sight of Allah, not beauty.

Remember, there's no right or wrong order for things to happen during puberty. Here are two beautiful hadith that will help you be content with your body and achieve a positive mindset towards comparing yourself to others. *Abu Huraira reported that the Messenger of Allah (saw) said, 'When one of you looks at someone who is better than him in wealth and physique, then he should look at one who is less well off than him.' (Sahih Muslim)*

Abu Huraira reported that the Messenger of Allah (saw) said, 'Look at those who are beneath you and do not look at those who are above you, for it is more suitable that you should not consider as less the blessing of Allah.' (Sunan Ibn Majah)

How you look

Feeling happy about how you look can help you to feel more positive. It's normal to worry about how you look sometimes. There can be a lot of pressure to look a certain way and fit in with everyone else. Sometimes you can be hurt or affected by what others think and say. You might feel unhappy about your hair, skin colour or weight or embarrassed about wearing hijab or braces. It can be hard to accept how you look if you feel pressure to have to look 'cute' to attract attention from boys.

Nude selfies

There's so much toxic competitiveness when you're a teenage girl; are my boobs smaller than hers? Is my skin fairer? Do boys like me more? Social media amplifies your anxieties, and society tells young women they must look sexy and act sexy. A recent Ofsted survey found boys regularly pressure girls to send nude selfies of themselves. Girls explained that if they blocked boys on social media, 'they just create multiple accounts to harass you'. The report also found nine in 10 girls believed that sexist name-calling and being sent unwanted explicit photos or videos happened 'a lot' or 'sometimes' between their peers. Sexual harassment has become normalised among school-age children. [36]

Your confidence can improve by not comparing yourself to girls you see on TikTok and Instagram. Remember, these edited images aren't authentic: no one looks that good in real life. And the beauty industry sells fantasy, not reality. So don't beat yourself up trying to look flawless. Sometimes other people can bully you, comment on your appearance or mistreat you. You could be told what to wear, or someone could try to make you look more like them. No one should make you feel bad about yourself. In healthy friendships, other people will accept you as you are.

Bullying

It can be tough if you're bullied because of your appearance. Being called names or treated badly because you are Muslim is also wrong. It's called Islamophobia. Being teased or discriminated against can make you want to change things about yourself. It might make you want not to wear hijab or talk about your beliefs. Racial bullying might make you want to wear makeup to change your skin tone. Remember, you don't have to change yourself to fit in. Getting support so that the racist or Islamophobic bullying can stop can help you to feel more confident. If you have been treated unfairly by your teachers or employers because you are Muslim then get advice about your rights from Cage.org[37] or Preventwatch.org.[38]

I know it's hard but talk to someone you trust, like a parent or older sibling, about what's happening. You're probably thinking that the bullying will get worse if I snitch on them. I'm not going to lie, it's true that could happen. But let me tell you something about what it means to be a Muslim: Muslims don't put up with bullying! We stand up for ourselves. People think Muslim girls are not assertive and easy to push around, but that's not true. We are not victims. We ask Allah to help us and act to change our situation. Bullies thrive on secrecy; they are the biggest cowards. If you don't expose them, they will continue to make your life hell and victimise other girls.

Seven things to think about

- Do dua, and ask Allah to help you feel content with your appearance.Negative or mean comments from boys or girls don't deserve your attention.

- Write down three things you like about yourself and read them every morning.

- Focus your energy on hobbies you enjoy or things you are good at - this can help build your confidence.

- Unfollow people who make you feel jealous. Reduce the time you spend with friends whose main pass time is backbiting. Look for more positive influences in your life.

- Wishing things are different won't change anything, and that time spent wishing is time you could spend changing what is in your control.

- Choose your friends wisely, keep company with Muslims who treat you well, Abu Musa reported: *The Prophet, (saw), said, 'Verily, the parable of good company and a bad company is only that of a seller of musk and a blacksmith. The seller of musk will give you some perfume, you will buy some, or you will notice a good smell. As for the blacksmith, he will burn your clothes or you will notice a bad smell.' (Muslim)*

- There is only one YOU so spend your time trying to become the best Muslim you can be!

ISLAMIC

SEX EDUCATION

O ur bodies are a remarkable gift given to us by Allah, and they are an amanah (trust), so only Allah can tell us what we can do with our bodies. We can experience a lot of fun and pleasure via our five senses, taste wonderful flavours, see breathtaking sights, and hear beautiful sounds. Furthermore, we can express love and affection by kissing and hugging our family and friends. Inshallah, in your lifetime, you will experience love in many forms, i.e. love for Allah, the Prophet (saw), your parents, siblings, extended family and the ummah.

Married couples

When you are ready for the responsibilities of family life, inshallah, you will look for a compatible god-conscious husband. When you find him, you will experience another dimension of love. Allah created love between husbands and wives and gave them a natural and pure desire to be close to each other and have children. One of the ways husbands and wives show their love and affection for each other is by kissing, hugging and having sexual intercourse or making love.

Muslims shouldn't talk about sex

Some Muslims consider any discussion about sex a violation of haha (modesty), unaware that the Prophet (saw) explained this subject in considerable detail. There is nothing wrong in gaining knowledge about this

136

subject as long as it is done with decency. Imam Bukhari relates from Mujahid, who said, *'Ilm (sacred knowledge) is not gained by a shy person nor an arrogant one.'* Similarly, he relates from Aisha, who said, *'How praiseworthy are the women of Ansar, shyness does not prevent them from having a deeper understanding of religion.'* *(Bukhari)*

Modesty is a fundamental characteristic of Islam. However, when it comes to sacred matters, it should not deter us from learning. In the West, questions of sexuality are discussed candidly and indecently. Why, then, should we feel ashamed of discovering the pure teachings of Islam on this subject? If you think the contents of this book are too direct, please keep in mind the words of Allah *'Surely, Allah is not shy of (expounding) the truth' (Al-Ahzab, 33:53).* Whatever is discussed in this book is based directly on Quran, Sunnah, sayings of the Companions of the Prophet and the four Sunni Schools of Islamic law. So bearing these hadith in mind, let's learn how we should understand sexual relations from an Islamic standpoint.

Why do people have sex?

There are a few reasons. People mainly have sex because it feels good. When Allah created the first human couple: our parents Adam and Hawa (as), he gave them the instinct to find the opposite gender attractive. Having sex within marriage is how Allah has enabled humans to satisfy that desire. Kissing and touching make couples feel sexually aroused, and they may have an orgasm, an intense feeling of pleasure across the body. Endorphins (a type of hormone) are released during an orgasm; they activate the pleasure centres in the brain, creating feelings of intimacy and relaxation.

Another reason people have sex is to have babies, so the human race continues to survive. Via the Quran, we can travel to the past to learn about the origins of humanity thousands of years ago.

Adam (as) the first human being

Allah tells us in the Quran that after He created everything on Earth, He created the seven heavens. He informed the angels that He intended to make man His representative (Khalifah) on Earth. *'Remember, O Prophet' when your Lord said to the angels, 'I am going to create a human being from clay. So when I have fashioned him and had a spirit of My Own 'creation' breathed into him, fall down in prostration to him.' (Sad,38:71-72)*

Using clay Allah formed Adam (as) and breathed life into him. Abu Musa relates in a hadith that Prophet (saw) said: *'Surely, Allah created Adam from clay selected from the different regions of the world. So, the children of Adam (the Banu Adam) went after the Earth – some of them turned out to be white, some red, some black and others between them. They turned out to be evil and good, and simple and tough, and there were those between the extremes.' (Ahmad)*

Adam (as) and Iblis

Allah taught Adam (as) the names of all things – knowledge that the angels didn't possess. He also gave him free will and all humans after him. This means that we have the choice to either obey or disobey Allah. Then Allah asked all the angels to bow to Adam (as). All the angels did so except Iblis. Iblis was a jinn, and he also had free will.

'He [Allah] said, 'What stopped you from prostrating when I commanded you?' He arrogantly replied, 'I am better than him: You created me from fire, while you created him from clay.' 'He [Allah] said, 'Then go down from here! It is not for you to show arrogance here, so go away! Surely you are one of those who are degraded. He appealed, "Then delay my end until the Day of their resurrection." Allah said, 'You are delayed ʾuntil the appointed Dayʾ.' He said, 'For leaving me to stray, I will lie in ambush for them on Your Straight Path. I will approach them from their front, their back, their right, their left, and then You will find most of them ungrateful.' Allah said, 'Get out of paradise! You are disgraced and rejected! I will certainly fill up Hell with you and your followers altogether.' (Al-Araf, 7:12-18)

So Iblis, also known as Shaytan, was cast away after he refused to obey Allah. Iblis then vowed to spend the rest of his days trying to lead humanity astray. When you read the tafsir of these ayat, you learn that Shaytan will ultimately go to jahanum (hell). He hates all humans because he blames our father, Adam (as), for his humiliation. And so he wants to have revenge on the Children of Adam (humankind) by taking as many of us with him to jahanum by persuading us to disobey Allah. Bear in mind that all he can do is whisper suggestions to us. He has no power to make us do anything.

Most of us don't intend evil, and Shaytan is very aware of this. So he distracts you, and he weakens your capacity to do good. He learns your weaknesses and uses them against you until you lose focus until you've immersed yourself in the dunya. Remember, he is an open enemy to you, and all that glitters is not gold. Shaytan works overtime to plant seeds of doubt in your mind. Allah knows your limits and your capacity to resist temptation so Allah tells you to steer clear of Shaytan's tricks for your own good. Know that even if you do not understand, there is always wisdom behind Allah's prohibitions. Seek refuge from Shaytan often and fortify yourself.[39]

Allah made all the Earth's creatures in pairs of male and female. He also created Hawa, the first woman and Adam's (as) wife. *'It is He Who created you from a single person and made his mate of like nature, in order that he might dwell with her in love...' (Al-Araf, 7:189)*. However, Shaytan managed to trick Adam and Hawa (as) into disobeying Allah.

ˈAllah said,ˈ 'O Adam! Live with your wife in paradise and eat from wherever you please, but do not approach this tree, or else you will be wrongdoers.' Then Satan tempted them in order to expose what was hidden of their nakedness. He said, 'Your Lord has forbidden this tree to you only to prevent you from becoming angels or immortals.' And he swore to them, 'I am truly your sincere advisor.' So he brought about their fall through deception. And when they tasted of the tree, their nakedness was exposed to them, prompting them to cover themselves with leaves from paradise. Then their Lord called out to them, 'Did I not forbid you from that tree and ˈdid I notˈ tell you that Shaytan is your sworn enemy?

'They replied, 'Our Lord! We have wronged ourselves. If You do not forgive us and have mercy on us, we will certainly be losers.' Allah said, 'Descend as enemies to each other.[humans and Shaytan]. You will find in the Earth a residence and provision for your appointed stay." He added, 'There you will live, there you will die, and from there you will be resurrected.' O children of Adam! We have provided for you clothing to cover your nakedness and as an adornment. However, the best clothing is

righteousness. This is one of Allah's bounties, so perhaps you will be mindful. O children of Adam! Do not let Satan deceive you as he tempted your parents out of paradise and caused their cover to be removed in order to expose their nakedness. Surely he and his soldiers watch you from where you cannot see them. We have made the devils allies of those who disbelieve.' (Al-Araf, 7: 19- 27)

Adam and Hawa

The whole of humankind descended from Adam (as) and Hawa (as), they are our parents, and we revere and respect them immensely. Adam (as) was also the first Prophet of Islam. They gave birth to many children. It is said that at each delivery, they had twins - a boy and a girl. They were commanded to marry the male of one set to the female of the next set and the male of that set to the female of the first, but they were not allowed to marry a brother and sister of the same birth. The marriage between sets of twins, an exception granted to the first generation of people, was for humanity to multiply.

'O mankind! Be careful of your duty to your Lord Who created you from a single soul, and from it created its mate, and from the two of them has scatted countless men and women [throughout the Earth]' (Al-Nisa,4:1)

Hawa (as) was created from the same soul as Adam (as), which means that she shared his fundamental human nature. Although she was differ-ent from Adam (as) physically, she had the same needs and instincts and intelligence. They complemented each other. All the world's people came from this first couple with their various nations, tribes, colours and lan-guages. All people on Earth make up the human race- and belong to the family of the Children of Adam.

141

Having the right intention

Muslims are only permitted to have sex when married. It is an intimate and powerful act. It creates a special bond between a couple. A wife and husband can have fun and enjoy sleeping together and being intimate. Did you know that a couple who intends to obey Allah and choose the halal way of making love will be rewarded for their actions?

The Prophet (saw) said, 'Actions are according to intentions, and everyone will get what was intended...' (Sahih Bukhari)

He (saw) also said: 'In the sexual act of each of you, there is a sadaqa.' The Companions replied: 'O Messenger of Allah! When one of us fulfils his sexual desire, will he be given a reward for that?' And he said, 'Do you not think that were he to act upon it unlawfully, he would be sinning? Likewise, if he acts upon it lawfully, he will be rewarded.' (Muslim)

Before we do an action we pause and consider our intentions rather than simply acting on our feelings and desires. It gives us time to reflect and determine whether Islam permits the activity we are about to engage in. Allah equipped us with a brain and a mind; therefore, unlike animals, we are not controlled by our instincts. The Quran instructs us to use our intelligence countless times.

Sexual Intercourse

Most probably, you are unmarried, but now is a good time to find out how the sexual act is performed and what actions are permitted. I shall refer to the body parts using scientific terminology. Also, whilst reading the explanation look at labelled scientific diagrams of the female and male reproductive systems. Refer to the glossary at the end of the book if there are words you do not understand.

Allah made men and women with different body parts inside and out. But they do have similarities as well. A woman's and a man's bodies are similar in specific ways. Both have a bladder for holding urine and a rectum for regulating solid waste. For both genders, their urine comes out through the urethra, and the solid waste comes out of the anus.

Female anatomy

Women have another opening called the vagina. Men are not born with vaginas. Further up inside a woman's body is the uterus. Allah has designed a woman's body to hold and grow a baby. The uterus is the unique place where a baby grows. The narrow bottom of the uterus is called the cervix. When a baby is ready to be born, this area opens up wider to make the baby come out through the vagina. It is incredible how Allah designed women to be the perfect home for a growing baby.

A woman's egg is part of what makes a baby; these eggs are very tiny. A woman's eggs are formed inside the ovaries. A woman has two ovaries. About once a month, an ovary releases an egg; this is called ovulation.

Male Anatomy

Men have a penis. Women are not born with penises. This organ hangs down from the front of a man's body. Another part of what makes a baby is a man's sperm; they are also very tiny. Sperm are produced in the testicles. Men have two testicles, just like women have two ovaries. Testicles are inside a layer of skin, and muscle called the scrotum; this hangs down underneath the penis. When a sperm from the man unites with an egg from the woman, this is called fertilisation.

For babies to be made, a husband and wife need to have sex. A man's penis is full of blood vessels. When he is getting ready to have sex, these blood vessels will fill with blood making his penis very hard and straight; this is called an erection. This allows him to insert his penis inside the woman's vagina. This is called having sex. It is how Allah designed us to feel close to the person we love and are married to and have babies with. It makes the husband and wife feel a special bond with each other.

Then the man's penis does something called ejaculation. This means a fluid called semen comes out of the penis. The semen contains lots of sperm. The sperm swims through the woman's body to get to the egg. If the woman's body has not released an egg at that time, the sperm will swim for a few days and eventually die.

But if the woman has released an egg, she could get pregnant. The sperm will swim up through the cervix into the uterus and then up through the fallopian tubes. Close to the ovary at the opening of the fallopian tube, an egg might be there for a sperm to fertilise. The sperm and egg combine their genetic material to make a new single living cell, which then grows into a baby inside the mother.

By the way, Islam does not say that every time a couple have sex, their intention should be to have a baby. They can use contraceptives such as condoms. Like with any action, a couple should research which form of birth control is permitted, and it should not negatively affect the wife or husband's health.

Pregnancy

Did you know that Allah speaks about pregnancy in the Quran over 40 times? The different stages of development of the fetus in the mother's womb are described in detail.

'And indeed, We created humankind from an extract of clay, then placed each 'human' as a sperm-drop in a secure place, then We developed the drop into a clinging clot 'of blood', then developed the clot into a lump 'of flesh', then developed the lump into bones, then clothed the bones with flesh, then We brought it into being as a new creation. So Blessed is Allah, the Best of Creators.' (Al-Muminun, 23:12-14)

Pregnancy is a wonderful experience, but let's be honest, it also involves morning sickness, sleepless nights and being poked and prodded by midwives and nurses. Having a supportive husband, in-laws and family is such a blessing. It's tough to go through a pregnancy and childbirth on your own.

In Surah Luqman, Allah does not shy away from describing the difficulties mother's face *'And We have commanded people to 'honour' their parents. Their mothers bore them through hardship upon hardship, and their weaning takes two years. So be grateful to Me and your parents. To Me, is the final return.' (Luqman, 31:14)*

Childbirth

Giving birth is the most difficult yet precious moment. This pregnancy stage in the Quran is shown in the case of Maryam (as), and Allah eased her pain by providing her with water and dates.

'So she [Maryam] conceived him [Isa] and withdrew with him to a remote place. Then the pains of labour drove her to the trunk of a palm tree. She cried, 'Alas! I wish I had died before this and was a thing long forgotten! So a voice reassured her from below her, 'Do not grieve! Your Lord has provided a stream at your feet. And shake the trunk of this palm

tree towards you; it will drop fresh, ripe dates upon you.' (Maryam, 19:22-25)

In movies, women in labour are often portrayed as going out of control, yelling and cursing their husbands. Muslims shouldn't act in that way. Although labour pains are excruciating (we are allowed to take pain relief), the Prophet (saw) tells us that anything that the believer experiences in terms of pain will wash away their sins: *'No misfortune or disease befalls a Muslim, no worry or grief or harm or distress – not even a thorn that pricks him – but Allah will expiate for some of his sins because of that.' (Bukhari)*

One of the most beautiful aspect of Islamic teachings is that mothers occupy a special place in Allah's eyes and that He sees and appreciates all of these struggles and sacrifices. As stated in the well-known hadith Prophet Muhammad (saw) said, *'Paradise lies beneath her [your mother's] feet.' (Ahmed)*

Some couples are unable to conceive and experience great sadness.They should seek medical assistance rather than blame each other. Furthermore, they can explore adoption as an alternative route to raising a family. I know many couples who have done this. Adopting and nurturing an orphan is very rewarding and a path to jannah.

Additionally, some women become pregnant but miscarry; I had a miscarriage, which was deeply traumatic. Others can suffer from post-natal depression. Getting help is essential, as Islam does not teach us to suffer in silence. Mental health issues are treatable and nothing to feel guilty or ashamed about. It can happen to anyone.

Alhamdulilah, Islam gives us a strategy for understanding such difficulties. Life is a test, and if we persevere and obey Allah, we will receive paradise as our eternal reward. Allah tells us He is the One` *'Who created death and life in order to test which of you is best in deeds. And He is the Almighty, All-Forgiving. (Al-Mulk, 67:2)*

Inshallah, you will want to get married and have children at some point in the future. But in the meantime, how should you interact with teenage boys and men at school or work? Can girls and boys be friends? What should you do if you have a crush on a boy in your class? Alhamdulillah, Allah and the Messenger have given us clear guidelines on gender relations. To begin with, Islam categorises the men/boys in your life as either your mahram or non-mahram.

A woman's mahram is a person she is never permitted to marry because of their close blood relationship, because they were breastfed by the same female relative or nursing maid, or because they become related through marriage.[40] The books of fiqh outline in detail the evidences for the complete list of mahrams which you can research. For now, here is a list of the ones mentioned in Surah al-Nur, where Allah says:

'... and not to reveal their adornment except to their husbands, or their fathers, or their husband's fathers, or their sons, or their husband's sons, or their brothers or their brother's sons, or their sister's sons...' (Al-Nur, 24:31)

1. Father, brothers and grandfathers.
2. Paternal uncles and maternal uncles.
3. Husband and husband's forefathers are mahrams by marriage, i.e. father-in-law.

4. Sons and grandsons, 'husband's sons' mentioned in the ayah, are the husband's sons from other wives, and these are her mahrams by marriage, not by blood.

5. Sisters and brothers sons.

6. Your cousins are NOT your mahram.

So your mahrams are the men you do not have to wear hijab in front of, and it is ok for you to socialise with. They are your male 'friends'. With all other boys and men, Muslim or non-Muslim, keep your relationship with them professional don't become friends. You can study, learn and work with teenage boys as colleagues but do not treat them as friends i.e. hanging out with them.

In numerous hadith, the Prophet (saw) instructed us to view fellow Muslims as part of the community that supports each other, '*Cooperate with one another in goodness and righteousness, and do not cooperate in sin and transgression. And fear Allah, for Allah is severe in punishment.*' *(Al-Maidah,5:2)*

Abu Musa reported: The Prophet (saw) said, 'Verily, the believers are like a structure, each part strengthening the other,' and the Prophet clasped his fingers together.' (Bukhari). This view seeks the good of a community governed by taqwa, not lust.

This respectful way cooperative way of viewing the opposite gender is the opposite of what non-muslim society teaches teenagers. The norm is for girls and boys to be boyfriends/girlfriends, flirt, go on dates, get bored of each other, break up and repeat the cycle again and again. You are seen as odd if you go against the tide. People like making fun of virgins. There is a lot of pressure to conform.

No one wants to be the odd one out. But young people also like to exaggerate, gossip and lie about who they have been with. 'I've done it lots of times. I lost it (virginity) when I was 15' 'It's amazing you don't know what you're missing' 'Everyones doing it' I understand it's difficult, especially as the hormones produced during puberty make you have sexual feelings, and it is natural to feel physically attracted to boys.

But just because you have these intense emotions doesn't mean you have to act upon them. It's peculiar how secular society teaches teenagers to desire sex without commitment. However, are you genuinely content living in this hyper-sexualised and carefree paradise? As believers, we are ever mindful of Allah, and insightfully, The Messenger of Allah (saw) said, *'The world is a prison for the believer and a paradise for the unbeliever.' (Muslim)*

Islam does not deny sexual pleasure but makes it lawful and private via marriage while ensuring people's well-being, safety and honour. The sacred texts provide ample evidence about how and when men and women can meet, how both genders should dress, and how we should respectfully treat each other. Many of the rulings in Islam protect us from sexual harassment, predators, and the temptation of zina (fornication) and promote modesty and chastity.

Here are just a few rules from Islam's social system that govern gender interactions. Studying this area further and reading the tafsir of the ayat mentioned will help you understand and implement the rules in your life.

Anas ibn Malik reported: The Messenger of Allah (saw) said: *'Seeking knowledge is an obligation upon every Muslim.' (Ibn Mājah)*

Men and women cannot meet in seclusion (khulwa)

Ibn Abbas said, *'I heard the Messenger of Allah (saw) give a sermon. He said, 'A man should not seclude himself with a woman except that there be with her someone who is of unmarriageable kin (mahram).' (Bukhari)*
Seclusion is defined as a man and a woman, who are not unmarriageable kin (mahram), being alone in an enclosed area so that a third party cannot easily enter upon them. Umar ibn al-Khattab narrated the Prophet (saw) said:

'Never is a man alone with a woman except that Shaytan is the third party with them.' (Tirmidhi)

So, going on a date where you will be alone in private with a man is not allowed. When this rule is applied, we can see how it would prevent sexual abuse from occurring inshallah. As a rule of thumb, do not be alone with any non-mahram, even if he is your cousin, Quran teacher or boss. You do not know his intentions or what Shaytan is whispering to him.

Men should lower their gaze

Men staring at women is creepy. Alhamdulilah, Allah protects women from unwanted attention. Allah says:
'Tell the believing men to lower their gaze (from looking at forbidden things) and protect their private parts (from illegal sexual acts, etc.). That is purer for them. Verily, Allah is All-Aware of what they do.' (An-Nur, 24:30)

Here is snippet of Ibn Kathir's tafsir of (24:30): The Prophet (saw) said,

'Beware of sitting in the streets.' They said, 'O Messenger of Allah, we have no alternative but to sit in the streets to converse with one another.' The Messenger (saw) replied, 'If you insist, then give the street its rights.' They asked, 'What are the rights of the street, O Messenger of Allah?' He said, 'Lower your gaze, return the greeting of salam, enjoin what is good and forbid what is evil.'

If men followed this guidance, it would discourage them from obsessively thinking about women as mere objects. In 2021, the murder of Sarah Everard and the outpouring of testimonies of sexual harassment in schools on the 'Everyone's Invited' website sharply bought into focus the massive problem of sexual harassment and violence against women and girls in the UK.

Men and women are instructed to keep certain parts of their bodies covered in public

Awrah refers to the intimate parts of the body that must be covered with clothing for both men and women. Exposing the awrah is unlawful and is regarded as a sin, except in situations of necessity, i.e., a medical examination. The awrah for a man in public refers to any part of the body between the navel and the knees. Whereas the awrah for a woman in public refers to the entire body except for the face and the hands.

When we restrict ourselves from looking at the awrah of men or women in person or images, we guard our chastity because what enters the eyes regularly is bound to find a place in one's heart and mind. In the voyeuristic societies we live in, there are multiple ways in which we've become progressively desensitised to pornographic content. For some, the casual glimpse on social media feeds eventually becomes an addiction.

Islam actively desexualises public life. In contrast, who can deny that Muslim and non-Muslim societies have become less civilised? Globally, the sexual revolution gave women more control and choice over their bodies. Still, it also ushered in the normalisation of self-objectification, and pornography, increased public immodesty, and an acceptance of relationships outside of marriage.

Women should lower their gaze and wear khimar and jilbab in public.

'And tell the believing women to lower their gaze. and be modest, and to display of their adornment only that which is apparent, and to draw their veils over their bosoms, and not to reveal their adornment save to their own husbands or fathers or husbands' fathers, or their sons or their husbands' sons, or their brothers or their brothers' sons or sisters' sons, or their women...' (An-Nur, 24:31)

'O Prophet! Ask your wives, daughters, and believing women to draw their cloaks over their bodies. In this way, it is more likely that they will be recognized `as virtuous` and not be harassed. And Allah is All-Forgiving, Most Merciful.'(Surah Ahzab, 33:59)

Please read Ibn Kathir's tafsir for a detailed explanation of both ayah. What you wear does matter. Feminists give young women the riskiest advice putting their fanaticism above girls' safety. 'Wear whatever you want. No one should tell you how to dress. Your body, your choice!' The message given to girls is dressing promiscuously is your right. Both genders make assumptions about each other based on their appearance. People will treat you differently depending on what you wear. We may not like it, but it's true. Let's not pretend we don't make assumptions about people based on what they are wearing.

Men are sexually aroused by women in revealing clothes. That does not give them the right to harass or assault a woman, but immoral men will do that if they think they can get away with it. Don't expect teenage boys fuelled by pornography to act like gentlemen. So please ignore the unsafe advice of feminists who expect men to have restraint or show girls any form of respect on the streets. Instead, obey Allah's commandments about dress code in public.

Unfortunately, we live in a hyper-sexualised world and women who are entirely covered are harassed, particularly in Muslim countries, but that isn't a reason to ignore Allah's laws; it illustrates how corrupt some men have become and why do Muslim governments not protected the honour of women by implementing Allah's laws?

Islam encourages marriage

Marriage fosters love and companionship between a husband and wife, promoting their happiness and respecting their complementary nature. Allah said: *'Among His signs is that He created for you mates from yourselves that you may find tranquillity in them, and He placed between you love and mercy. Verily, in that are signs for a people who give thought.' (Ar-Rum,30:21)*

Aisha reported: The Messenger of Allah (saw) said, *'Marriage is part of my Sunnah. Whoever does not act upon my Sunnah is not part of me.*

Give each other in marriage, for I will boast of your great numbers before the nations. Whoever has the means, let him contract a marriage. Whoever does not have the means should fast, as fasting will restrain his impulses.' (Sunan Ibn Mājah)

Islam has forbidden sexual relations outside of marriage

'It is lawful for you to marry chaste Muslim women and chaste women of the People of the Book, provided you pay their dowry, maintain chastity, and avoid fornication or lustful relations outside of marriage. The deeds of anyone who rejects the faith certainly, become fruitless. He will be of those who lose on the Day of Judgment.' (Al-Maidah, 5:5)

Sexual abuse is haram

Sexual abuse is when someone is forced, pressured or tricked into participating in sexual activity with another person. It could be online or in person and can happen to anyone. Sexual abuse includes:

- Someone flashing or exposing themselves to you in person or online.
- Being pressured or told to share sexual images or videos of yourself.
- Being sent, shown or given sexual pictures and videos, including porn
- Being given gifts and then made to feel like you owe someone something sexual.

Talking about sexual abuse can feel difficult sometimes, but you should never have to cope alone. Telling someone what's happened can help you get support and stop what's happening. If you've been sexually abused and you're not sure how to talk about it, it can help to:

- Pick someone you trust, an adult in your family; if they do not believe you or help you, tell another adult. Do not let the perpetrator get away with it.
- Writing a letter saying things aloud can be hard, but writing it down can help. You could write a letter. Having a letter can be a good way to start a conversation.
- Think of a time when you can talk privately or ask the person you trust for some time to speak. You could also choose a safe way to give them your letter.

Homosexual and lesbian relationships are forbidden

Homosexuality is the sexual interest in and attraction to members of one's own sex. The term *gay* is frequently used as a synonym for homosexual; female homosexuality is referred to as lesbianism. Gay men have sex by inserting their penis into the anus of another man. This was the action of the accursed people of the Prophet of Allah Lut (as).

Lesbians have sex by inserting their fingers or other objects into another woman's vagina. They both go against the fitrah (natural disposition) that Allah has created in humans and animals, whereby the male is inclined towards the female and vice versa. Non-Muslims have normalised this behaviour, and they want Muslims to accept it is ok, but Allah tells us in the Quran homosexuality is a serious sin, and he punishes people who act upon same-sex attraction:

'And (remember) Lut! When he said to his people, 'Do you commit Al-Fahishah (evil, great sin, every kind of unlawful sexual intercourse, sodomy) while you see (one another doing evil without any screen)? Do you practice your lust on men instead of women? Nay, but you are a people who behave senselessly.' There was no other answer given by his people except that they said: 'Drive out the family of Lut from your city. Truly, these are men who want to be clean and pure!' So We saved him and his family, except his wife. We destined her to be of those who remained behind. And We rained down on them a rain (of stones). So evil was the rain of those who were warned.' (Al-Naml 27:54-58)

We are commanded to stay away from shamelessness

There are three words for shamelessness used in the Quran.

- Al fahsha: This refers to shamelessness in the general sense, the idea of being inappropriate or doing ugly things. Anything ugly, detestable behaviour is considered fahsha: socially unacceptable speech, clothing, or actions. Vulgarity, lewdness, etc., fall under fahsha.

- Al fahisha: This refers to a particular act of inappropriateness.

- Al fawahish: The plural for both, it includes both al fahsha and al fahisha.

'Indeed, Allah commands justice, grace, as well as courtesy to close relatives. He forbids shamelessness (al fahsha), wickedness, and aggression. He instructs you, so perhaps you will be mindful.' (An-Nahl, 16:90)

'And come not near to unlawful sex (avoid all situations that might possibly lead to it.). Verily, it is a fahishah (immoral sin) meaning a major sin' (Al-Isra, 17:32)

If you have friends that are guys, very quickly you lose your sense of modesty; privacy goes out of the window, sending suggestive selfies becomes acceptable, and your texts become more flirtatious. Speaking about prohibited things becomes normalised. Where does it end? When you lose your sense of shame, you are no longer ashamed in front of Allah. Allah warns us: *'Shaytan threatens you with poverty and orders you to commit fahsha (evil deeds, illegal sexual intercourse, sins, etc.) whereas Allah promises you Forgiveness from Himself and Bounty, and Allah is All-Sufficient for His creatures' needs, All-Knower.' (Al-Baqarah, 2:268)*

Ibn Masood (ra) said that the Prophet (saw) said: *'Among that which reached the people from the words of the earlier prophethood: If you feel no shame, then do whatever you wish.' (Bukhari)*

In contrast, western societies encourage shamelessness by focusing on the individual's rights and freedoms as long as their actions do not harm others. Unfortunately, this is a global problem that also affects the Muslim world. Besides, in a capitalist economy, sex has become commodified and transactional. Where there is consumer demand for a product, companies will supply it. Selling sex is acceptable in a capitalist economy because there is a demand despite apparent detrimental effects on individuals and the wider society. For example, in 2015, the pornography industry was estimated to be worth $97 billion.

Most capitalist economies have minimal state regulations, so nothing stops multinational companies from using sexual images to sell their goods. With their multi-million-dollar marketing budgets and militia of psychologists, global corporations are conditioning us to be compliant consumers who accept this sexualisation. Our well-being is not the prime motivating factor. Rather self-interest and maximising profit are.

The problem is that we do not choose whether to live in a hyper-sexualised society where our desires are constantly being manipulated. Wouldn't you prefer that women and men were represented with respect in society? Instead of the female body, in particular, being presented sexually for consumption. We don't need to ape the Tinder culture of non-Muslims, a culture that has created a generation of sex-obsessed commitment-phobes. We need to be smart and accept the guidance of our Creator:

'This day, I have perfected your religion for you, completed My Favour upon you, and have chosen for you Islam as your religion' (Al-Maidah,5:3).

GENDER IDENTITY AND LGBTQIA+

Wanting to understand your identity and where you fit in is a natural part of growing up. It's a time when there are many opportunities to learn about yourself, so to ask the question, 'Who am I?' is entirely normal. Your identity is composed of beliefs, experiences, and relationships that give you a sense of who you are. Along with traits like ethnicity, gender, class, and nationality, it also includes political opinions, moral attitudes, and religious beliefs, all of which guide your day-to-day choices and actions.

Identify yourself

You may view yourself as a student, Muslim, daughter, sister, a woman of colour, working class, opposed to animal cruelty, pro-Palestinian, and anti-racist. Given your complex personality. Which ideas should you embrace to shape your identity? If you live in a non-Muslim country, you will be given the following flawed advice.

- Experimentation is an integral part of finding out who you are. There is no right or wrong. But you should not break the law.

- It's ok to try different identities regarding appearance, studies, work, gender, sexuality, and lovers to see what fits and what's 'just not me.'

- You must develop an authentic self - the true self - distinct from your parents to flourish as an independent adult.

- If a belief or idea makes you feel conflicted and does not align with your true self, it's ok to reject it. You do you!

Based on this poor advice, if you aren't sure whether you prefer guys or girls, sleep with both and decide based on how satisfied you feel. You don't have to follow your religion or your parents if they disagree with your choices because you are independent, and they cannot impose their beliefs on you. And if you need help, find the answers on TikTok or Youtube from equally confused teenagers with similar 'lived experience'.

Teenage drama

It's odd how liberal society teaches teenagers to desire sex without commitment. But how is this pleasure-seeking life advice working for young people in the West? Unfortunately, many American teenagers – particularly girls – are unhappy with their lives and are facing depression.[41]

'Anxiety and depression aren't the only concerns for U.S. teens. Smaller though still, substantial shares of teens in the Pew Research Center survey say drug addiction (51%) and alcohol consumption (45%) are major problems among their peers.'[42]

Teenage girls face increasing levels of sexual assault. According to a study in the U.K., one in three teenage girls has suffered sexual abuse from a boyfriend, and one in four has experienced violence in a relationship.

One of the report's authors, Professor David Berridge of Bristol University, said: 'The high rate and harmful impact of violence in teenagers' intimate relationships, especially for girls, is appalling…It was shocking to find that exploitation and violence in relationships starts so young. 'Sian, one of the girls who was interviewed for the research, said: 'I only went out with him for a week. And then, because I didn't want to have sex, he just started picking on me and hitting me.'[43]

Sexual assault

Today it is difficult for young women to express dissatisfaction with the premise of the sexual arrangement that society expects them to make. This arrangement instructs you to forego your well-being to indulge your hedonistic desires and stay competitive in the dating market. But casual sex is a risky pass time. Rape and sexual harassment are ubiquitous. While the frequency of rape varies by state, it averages one every 1-2 minutes in the United States. In addition, in the United States, 70% of rapes are committed by someone the victim knows. Astonishingly, it is estimated that approximately 35% of women worldwide have experienced sexual harassment at some point in their lives.[44]

Tragically, women are being sexually assaulted in the twenty-first century more than ever before. Politicians and the police only pay lip service to protect women. Additionally, society instils in young girls the notion that it is acceptable to go to a club, get drunk, dance and flirt with a complete stranger, and then go to his apartment and have sex with him. There isn't anything more immoral and risky to teach young women. An oft-repeated solution to this problem is 'Don't teach girls not to get raped. Teach boys not to rape.' This is correct but ignores the mixed messages both genders send each other. And more importantly, it fails to question the driving force behind predatory behaviour: individual freedom.

161

Individual freedom is gold

The only restriction on personal liberty is that you should not cause harm to another person. But who will enforce that 'harm principle' when two people are alone in a locked bedroom, in the backseat of a car, or drunk in a dimly lit nightclub? How can a woman prove she did not consent with no witnesses? How can a man prove he is not a rapist? A perfect storm has been created. Predators do not fear the law. The fear of God has vanished. So, what remains? Personal morality is founded on secular individualism.

Like, pick and mix men and women choose which rules to follow and which to ignore based on what makes them 'happy'. Sex education lessons teach boys to respect women, whereas hyper-sexualised music videos teach the opposite. Their girlfriends will say, 'Don't treat me like a sex object!' but their social media feeds are flooded with women objectifying themselves.

The letter of the law says it's a crime to rape a woman, but most rapists escape punishment. In the U.S., for instance, it is estimated that only 9% of rapists are prosecuted, and only 3% spend time in prison. 97% of rapists walk free.[45]

Sexual Revolution

Did the Sexual Revolution not inspire people to reject religion and go beyond normal sexual behaviour? Yes, it did. And so the genie is out of the bottle and cannot be put back in. Teenagers often engage in underage drinking, underage unprotected sex, and cannabis use. It has become commonplace to break the law, and the police turn a blind eye. Therefore, just about everyone sets their own rules when it comes to 'love'.

Both sexes have been socialised to believe that sexual promiscuity is a fundamental human right. In the United States, there were '2.5 million documented cases of chlamydia, gonorrhoea, and syphilis' in 2021.[46] That number alone should cause women to pause and consider whether the mindset of engaging in risky sex is beneficial to their health.

LGBTQIA+

As you are aware, discussions about gender identity and LGBTQIA+ are everywhere. To my eye, confusion about sexuality and gender exists because, since the 1960s Sexual Revolution, many in the West believe that people should be free to love whomever they want. Casual sex and dating are not considered sinful. Pornography is now commonplace, and same-sex relationships are acceptable.

From a young age, liberal society teaches everyone that it is ok to be different. You are an individual; love has no gender, and no labels. Teenagers are saturated with an avalanche of LGBTQIA+ propaganda in movies, music, and social media. Few voices in mainstream culture offer a counter-narrative. As a result, many young people believe that their sexuality and gender are the most critical aspects of their identity.

What exactly is sexuality?

Sexuality refers to the people you are sexually and romantically attracted to. Most people on the planet are heterosexual: men are attracted to women, and women are attracted to men. The acronym LGBTQIA+ encompasses other identities. A lesbian is a woman who is attracted to women. A gay man is attracted to men. A bisexual person is attracted to both men and women. Islam prohibits homosexuality, (evidences are provided in the sex education chapter) and we should not consume entertainment that normalises such behaviour; otherwise, slowly, we will begin to think it's acceptable.

What is gender?

Medical staff record whether we are a girl or boy when we are born based on our reproductive organs. A tiny minority of babies are born with both male and female organs and are recorded as intersex. Since the beginning of time, people have felt comfortable with the gender recorded at birth.

Humanity was divinely created from a male and a female, as stated in the Quran, which reads, *'O Mankind! We created you from a male and a female...' (Hujurat, 49:13).* Additionally, Allah clearly asserts that there are only two sexes in humanity: *'...and from the two of them, He spread forth multitudes of men and women' [Nisa: 1), and 'And the male is not like the female...' (Al Imran: 36)*

Gender is not a social construct

A number of Islamic legal and social judgments, are different for men and women, and many aspects of our Islamic Shariah are essentially gender-based. Declaring that gender is a social construct with no natural connection to biological sex is just false. Male and female genes are different from one another. The Shariah established each gender's duty and obligations because males and females differ in so many ways—physically, biologically and emotionally.

Men pretending to be women

Since the beginning of time people have been content with their natural gender. Today, you have people who want to choose their gender-based purely on their subjective feelings rather than the objective reality of their biology. They are called transgender and adopt the mannerisms and clothes of the opposite sex. It's called gender self-identification, and it is a modern problem.

Caitlyn Jenner, born William Bruce Jenner, is probably the most famous example of a man who self-identifies as a trans-woman. After undergoing extreme plastic surgery to create a fake vagina, Jenner tweeted, 'I'm so happy after such a long struggle to be living my true self.'[47] Another famous example is the actor Laverne Cox. Men such as Jenner and Cox, who think their gender identity differs from what was recorded at birth, are diagnosed with having gender dysphoria, also known as gender identity disorder.

Transitioning is traumatic

Gender transitioning is the process that a transgender person chooses to go through to alter their appearance. It is a mentally and physically harrowing process involving lifelong drug dependency and years of extreme plastic surgery. How can a person expect to achieve contentment when they are going against the will of Allah? But that's what happens when choice becomes god.

For a man to look like a woman, he must take oestrogen for the rest of his life to stop his body from producing testosterone. Most men go under the knifed to have brow lifts, liposuction, nose reshaping, breast augmentation, tracheal shave, cheek implants, lip lift, lip and cheek implants, cheek softening, and face/neck lifts. Some have a penile inversion, a serious, sometimes fatal cosmetic procedure in which the penis is turned inside out to create the inner walls of the vagina.[48] Obviously, the man will always have to wear excessive make-up to keep up the facade.

Pharmaceutical companies, the make-up industry, plastic surgeons and therapists are making a lot of money from transgender people. And so, it is also to their benefit to promote transgender ideology and look for new customers I.e teenagers and kids.

Most teenagers naively think 'trans rights' means trans want equal treatment and access to toilets and changing rooms because they are a discriminated minority. But here's a question when you see a trans-woman on the street, do you instinctively know they are not a woman? Everyone does because Allah created us with the ability to recognise other people's sex. But the trans fanatics and self-identification bigots want you to throw your instincts in the river and demand you validate their feelings and chosen gender. But why should you?

Trans people are not 'born that way'
A new report from Sanjana Friedman at Pirate Wires documents a phenomenon that for some men, the solution to the despair of living as an isolated, unhappy male is straightforward: become a woman. They call themselves 'transmaxxers' and they believe gender transition can be an effective tool for escaping the misery of involuntary celibacy, social isolation, and professional mediocrity.[49]

So the subculture of young men embrace trans identities not because they believe they were born in the wrong body but simply because they can, and because they think living as a woman will make their lives better.[50] Tina, a German trans-woman, explains how she did this 'I had never concerned myself with any kind of trans stuff before,' Tina told me, referencing her mindset prior to her decision to transmaxx. But after going to several trans-specialised psychologists and telling her 'completely fake' dysphoria story — 'the general gist of it is, 'I've had gender dysphoria since I was 14... I'm uncomfortable around women and I envy them for their femaleness and all that kind of s***' — she received a diagnosis of gender dysphoria and prescriptions for anti-androgens and oestrogen.'[51]

Tina's honest admission reveals more nakedly than ever before the true face of the LGBTQIA+ ideology. It has nothing to do with being born this way; it is solely about personal pleasure-seeking. There are many more examples in Friedman's report of men faking symptoms of gender dysphoria. Fundamentally, there is no way a person can prove they are in the wrong body, it's all about how they feel.

Why are children changing their gender?

What is even more worrying is how minors are being taught this self-identification belief system in schools. It is causing them a great deal of confusion and anxiety. Here is an example, 'Hi, my name is Elise. I've used she/her pronouns all my life. But recently, and for a while, I've been struggling with gender issues as well as a whole lot of other identity things. So, I finally gave in and ordered a [breast] binder for myself and it just came in today.'[52]

Adults are supposed to provide youngsters with clear intelligent objective guidance. Instead they are telling kids 'You are the best expert of your identity, you can choose your gender.' Following the modern script, teenagers have learnt never to say, 'I've decided to be trans', because my friends are trans and I feel left out, but always, 'I've discovered that I am trans.'[53]

Islam forbids transgenderism and cross-dressing

Ibn' Abbas reported: The Prophet (saw) cursed the effeminate men and the masculine women. He said: *'Turn them out of your houses.' (Bukhari)*. All mainstream fiqh scholarly bodies worldwide deem it impermissible to actively attempt to change one's biological sex/ gender through hormone treatment, surgical procedures, or any combination of the two. All mechanisms for seeking to actively transition from one sex/gender to another are forbidden according to the teachings of Islam.[54]

'The origins of this belief system date back almost a century, to when doctors first sought to give physical form to the yearnings of a handful of people who longed to change sex. For decades such 'transsexuals' were few and far between, the concern of a handful of maverick clinicians who would provide hormones and surgeries to reshape their patients' bodies to match their desires as closely as possible... They used to be the exception.'[55]

Women only safe spaces are targeted by trans

In the west, the exception has changed into the rule since the turn of the century. Laws and policies relating to store changing rooms, toilets, school curricula, swimming pools, prisons, and gyms are being changed to favour self-declared gender identity over biological gender. Equality campaigners say the objective is inclusivity. No one should be made to feel different. But women and girls are being put in danger to accommodate the feelings of men who claim womanhood.

Unisex changing rooms are unsafe

Data from the Sunday Times revealed that most sexual assaults at public swimming pools in the U.K. happen in unisex changing rooms. 90 per cent of assault, voyeurism and harassment cases relate to the gender-neutral zones, which have been branded a 'magnet' for sexual predators. Of 134 complaints in the U.K. last year, 120 were about incidents in unisex changing rooms... These figures show that women and girls are more vulnerable in mixed changing rooms.'[56]

This is the condescending advice the University of Bristol LGBT+ Society offers to female students who are worried about their safety, 'If you're in a public bathroom and you think a stranger's gender doesn't match the sign on the door, follow these steps: 1. Don't worry about it, they know better than you.'

The objective of having women-only toilets and shower rooms has always been to protect girls and women from harassment and sexual violence. The United Nations and NGOs such as Save the Children and ActionAid advocate for women-only toilets in schools in the developing world, knowing that without them, teenagers are more likely to be molested or raped.

Trans-activists don't care about women's safety

But trans-activists often reject concerns that men who identify as women may abuse or assault females by accessing women-only spaces and services. After all, transwomen are women, they argue, and if you disagree, you are a prejudiced transphobe.

Charlotte Kirby, 25, posted a sobbing video to TikTok in September 2022

describing how two men pulled back the curtain in different incidents while she was trying on clothes at the Primark store in Cambridge. Primark stores no longer have separate male and female changing rooms, instead allowing all shoppers to try on clothes in
individual cubicles beside one another.

In the video, Ms Kirby said: 'I was trying on some clothes and it was a unisex changing room - which, I'm all for and I love that because it makes everyone feel included. But twice men opened the curtain and walked in on me. Luckily, both times I was wearing clothes but I could easily not have been.I just want to say to everyone to please be careful. And if you are going to a changing room, don't go in on your own. I know I will never be doing that again.' 57

Thankfully Charlotte Kirby was not physically attacked by either man. Just imagine if that had happened to you. Why are the safety and interests of young women being ignored and devalued? Nicola Williams, the spokeswoman for Fair Play for Women, said: 'Spaces, where women are undressed, should be single-sex as a matter of course. This is obvious, elementary safeguarding.'58

Trans-women attack women jail

You'll be surprised to find that male inmates in the UK have been able to request to be transferred to a women's jail since 2016. All they have to do is identify as female. Permission to transfer does not require a legal or medical transition, which means that legally-male prisoners, complete with male genitalia, are already living in jail alongside women.

We have prisons for male prisons and separate prisons for female prisoners. In the past, a male rapist would never be put in a female prison because it would be dangerous and intimidating for the women. But thanks to this new progressive way of viewing gender, that is precisely what is happening, and male-bodied transgender women are assaulting real women in jail.

'A predatory and controlling rapist has been jailed for life after she attacked vulnerable women in female prisons. Karen White (Stephen Terence Wood) 52, who was described as being a danger to women and children, admitted sexually assaulting women in a female prison and raping another two women outside jail.'[59]

Many female prisoners are incredibly vulnerable. Countless women have been victims of male sexual exploitation and abuse. Consider what it must be like for women who have been victims of male violence to then be in prison with men. Male prisoners claiming a female gender identity should not be sent to women's prisons on demand; instead, there should be transgender wings. Richard Garside of the Centre for Crime and Justice Studies raises an important point, 'My concern about the current approach is that it is appears to privilege the subjective feelings of particular, largely male, prisoners at the expense of the needs of those prisoners, largely women, who have to live with the decisions imposed upon them.'

Non-binary
Some people call themselves non-binary, which means they are saying they are neither male nor female or feel they are both. This does not make sense as everyone is born with a biological sex. Pretending you are not a man or woman is childish. Non-binary, gender fluid, they/them pronouns: it all sounds rather harmless. This sounds like a simple opting

out of gendered expectations, perhaps even a positive move. So why should you care?

Did you know resources and facilities that are supposed to be just for young women like you are being taken away by men pretending they are not men? 'Opting out of being legally male will confer the right to access women-only spaces such as female-only changing rooms and female-only sports? That is what trans lobby groups are asking for. There is a growing expectation that 'non-binary' people belong in women's spaces - even though they say they are not women-.We are already seeing women-only scholarships and sports stating that trans and non-binary people are welcome.' [60]

How to view your identity

The most fundamental aspect of your identity is your belief in 'la ilaha illallah muhammadur rasool allah'. That there is no deity but Allah, and Muhammad is the messenger of Allah. Your identity is built on the foundations of the teachings of the Quran and Sunnah.

Your gender or sexuality is not your defining feature. It's just one aspect of you. In Islam, all people are born equal in Allah's eyes, and the only trait that distinguishes one person from another is righteousness, taqwa. *'O people, We have created you male and female and made you into nations and tribes that you may know one another. Verily, the noblest of you to Allah is the most righteous of you. Verily, Allah is knowing and aware.' (Al-Hujurat, 49:13)*

When a person doesn't accept the guidance of Allah, they will never know their true purpose in life. They will make feeling happy the purpose of their life. Allowing their desires to be their guide. Jump from one high to another. Never feeling content, constantly buying new things, optimising their appearance, sexual partners and now gender.

Taqwa is the only quality that makes someone exceptional in the sight of Allah, not gender. The essence of our religion is to control our desires and bring them in line with the Shariah; desires do not define a person, and conquering urges contrary to our faith is how
piety is established. Inshallah, to gain a more detailed understanding of the Islamic rulings related to LGBTQIA+, please read the fatwa prepared by Dr Yasir Qadhi in 2022 for the Fiqh Council of America, which is available online.[61]

FASHION VICTIMS

odest fashion: it's a goldmine. According to the Global Islamic Economic Report, women's modest fashion accounted for
$44 billion in sales in 2015 and shows no signs of abating.
By 2025, it's estimated to be worth $88bn.[62] These figures reveal why
global brands want to get their hands on our hijabs! Gucci and Nike have
been marketing hijabs since 2018. Dolce & Gabbana launched a lavish
collection of abayas back in 2016. And in 2019, Sports Illustrated surprisingly showcased figure-hugging burkinis declaring, 'whether you are
wearing a one-piece, a two-piece, or a burkini, you are the pilot of your
own beauty.'

Their PR peddles individuality and empowerment, but we know 'it's all
about the money, money, money.' But wait, there's more! In 2021, United
Colours Of Benetton launched what is being deemed as a progressive
innovation, a 'unisex hijab' designed by Italian rap star Ghali. And Tom-
my Hilfiger has recently launched its latest accessory – the hijab – complete with its iconic initials 'TH' branded into the fabric.

Modest fashion is a double-edged sword. I used to live in Istanbul: the
modest fashion capital of the world and it was so good to be able to find
elegant, full-length dresses and matching scarves. This is partly due to
the global fashion industry waking up to the lucrative opportunity of
modest fashion. Muslimahs no longer have to choose between being
fashionable or modest: we can have both. We are having our cake and
eating it. It's okay to look put together.

But can we overlook the not-so-palatable consequences of the modest
fashion movement? Thirty or so years ago, the term modest fashion did

not exist. If you wanted to wear hijab and jilbab, you would either make them yourself, buy them from an Islamic shop or get them from a Muslim country. Your options were limited; to be honest, being fashionable was not the priority: obeying Allah was. We knew there was a time and place to be attractive and gorgeous, and that was in the private sphere. Veteran hijabis look back at that era with nostalgia...

So what was the game changer? Well, it was a combination of hijabi fashion bloggers, Muslim designers, faith-influenced fashion brands and social media. Mainstream brands were neglecting Muslim women, so designers and fashionistas started their own clothing lines, showed women how to style their scarves and adapt clothes to make them adhere to Islamic requirements. Once the big brands realised there were big bucks to be made in modest wear, they opportunistically jumped on the bandwagon.

Today, western brands are the driving force in the modest fashion world. We see the Hilfiger hijab and think, 'Yes! Muslim representation. Finally, I am being seen' But here's the problem. 'Branded hijabs invite women who want to live in a world full of commodities to seek the fantasy of status elevation through their proximity with designer labels. Designer labels embellish the the hijab with the illusion of worldly gain. In so doing, they secularise it.'[63]

They have hijacked the 'Islamic roots' of modest fashion and replaced it with rampant consumerism, and Muslim women are now their target consumers. As targets, we are being stripped away from Islamic influences that may allow us to make rational clothing choices. A 'liberated' woman, and an 'autonomous' teenager, are all susceptible to the power of advertisers.

Family and religion help us make better decisions - but without these, or if you can lessen the influence parents or people of knowledge - then left alone, you become a creature of consumption. Halima Aden, the world's first hijab-wearing supermodel, wishes she had listened to her mother's pleas 'to open [her] eyes and quit modelling a LONG time ago. I wish I wasn't so defensive,'[64]

This is what Durkheim called anomie, the breakdown of structures of guidance and norms. 'Anomie is a sense of alienation and hopelessness in a society or group that is often a response to social upheaval. This causes the breakdown of an individual's usual social or ethical standards.'[65]

There is a reason why DKNY, ASOS, and Mango marketers don't use the phrase 'khimar', 'jilbab' or 'niqab' in their marketing: it would be a PR disaster. These words have a specific definition in an Islamic framework. In contrast, the term 'modesty' is open to personal interpretation, an expression of individuality: exactly how modern consumer capitalism wants Muslims to view their clothing. So, our hijab is being reimagined by non-Muslim fashion brands and then aggressively marketed to us.

Modesty is mentioned in the Quranic verses that prescribe hijab: *'And say to the believing women that they should lower their gaze and guard their modesty; that they should not display their beauty and ornaments except what must ordinarily appear therof; that they should draw their veils over their bosoms...' (An-Nur, 24:31)*

But let's not forget, fundamentally, we wear hijab as an act of worship alone solely for the sake of Allah, and inshallah, we will be rewarded for our obedience. No one denies that the Islamic dress code conceals our bodies. But modesty is a relative expression, different for everyone depending on their cultural practice. On the other hand, Islam has defined with precision how and which areas of a woman's body should be covered. Hence, modesty is not the criterion for choosing what we wear: the Shariah is.

Aisha Hasan, the founder of the Qarawiyyin Project, notes 'It would be naïve to not also recognise that many Muslim women have used the idea of modesty alone to dictate how they should dress, arguing that it is the spirit, not the specifics of the Islamic dress-code, that is important.'[66]

This idea that we only have to follow the spirit rather than the letter of Islamic law is just plain wrong. If it were correct, then why not apply it to the dietary rules in Islam? This thinking would make drinking wine and pork acceptable.

As mentioned earlier, the fashion industry encourages rampant consumerism and environmentally unfriendly throw-away fashion, which Islam does not condone. The fashion industry thrives on discontent, making us desire what is trending. Islam instructed us to be presentable, but we don't need to overhaul our wardrobes every season.

Furthermore, it's sad to see Muslim fashion brands perpetuating the same unrealistic euro-centric beauty standards by opting for tall, fair, slim, airbrushed models. I know clothes hang better on thin stick models; I have read 'The Beauty Myth'. But where is the diversity? Why are they using unethical marketing techniques to sell clothing to Muslims? Not only that, we've all heard of the marketing motto 'sex sells', and so we are witnessing the blatant sexualisation of hijab and Muslim models on catwalks.

One of the many reasons Halima Aden cited for quitting runway shows was, 'I eventually drifted away and got into the confusing grey area of letting the team on-set style my hijab... I trusted the team on set to do my hijab, and that's when I ran into problems,' she said, adding, 'like jeans being placed on my head in place of a regular scarf...My hijab kept shrinking and got smaller and smaller with each shoot.' The former model also spoke about a 'horrendous' magazine cover that made her look like a 'white man's fetishised version of me'. She also said she felt pressure from other Muslim women to be more daring and tried to be 'the hot hijabi as if that didn't just defeat the whole purpose.'

Like sheep to the slaughter, we consume, like and applaud these provocative sexualised images, and perversely we emulate them. Like Muslim models, we are expected to obey the fashion gurus. Those who do not adopt the modest fashion industry's version of hijab are made to feel frumpy and represent a traditional Islam that has failed to keep up with modernity.

Do you think we may have been too hasty in embracing the modest fashion movement uncritically? Compliant consumers, god forbid, fashion victims mesmerised by the allure of being on-trend and garnering compliments for our unique style. What have we lost at the altar of fashion? Are we following in the footsteps of the vain emperor in his new clothes?

Have we been persuaded to reject our khimar and jilbabs in exchange for turbans, skinny jeans and individuality?

In January 2023, Batul Bazzi, a famous fashion influencer based in the United States, deleted images from Instagram and TikTok as she no longer wanted to promote content that was not Islam-focused. Batul stated, 'I want to level up with my modesty' and does not want to keep 'promoting an image of myself that does not align with who I am on the inside.' Alhamdulillah, it's heartening to see more and more Muslimahs discarding the 'fashion victim mindset' and embracing an Islamic perspective on fashion.

Today, fashion designers and models have too much influence: Rihanna, Bella Hadid, Kylie Jenner, Calvin Klein etc., are literally worshipped in the west. Secular liberalism encourages people to become obsessed with themselves, their beauty, their bodies their clothes. They are so fixated on their outer appearance because this life means everything. They have no other purpose in life. We don't want to follow in their footsteps. Islam encourages us to be beautiful and stylish but within limits set by our Creator, not His creation.

Abdullah ibn Mas'ud said that the Prophet (saw) said, *'No one will enter Paradise who has an atom's weight of pride in his heart.' A man said, 'What if a man likes his clothes to look good and his shoes to look good?' He said, 'Allah is beautiful and loves beauty. Pride means denying the truth and looking down on people.' (Muslim)*

We must also bear in mind the hadith in Sahih Muslim where the Prophet (saw) said, *'Allah does not look at your outward appearance and your wealth, rather He looks at your hearts and deeds.' (Bukhari)*

So, Allah wants us to beautify our tongues with the truth. Our hearts with sincere devotion (ikhlas), love, repentance and obedience. Beautify our bodies by showing His blessings upon us in our clothing. We should recognise Allah through these qualities of beauty and seek to draw close to Him through beautiful words, deeds and attitudes.

In Sunan at-Tirmidhi, it says, *'Allah loves to see the effects of His blessing on His slave.'* It was reported that Abul-Ahwas al-Jashami said the Prophet (saw) saw him wearing old, tattered clothes and asked him, *'Do you have any wealth?' I said, 'Yes.' He said, 'What kind of wealth?' I said, 'All that Allah has given me of camels and sheep.' He said, 'Then show the generous blessings that He has given you.'*

Following the prophetic tradition will help us develop a healthy balanced attitude towards style and spirituality, and reading the tafsir of the ayat regarding clothing will prevent us from compromising our religious beliefs. Inshallah, never forget, my dear sister: we are slaves of Allah, not slaves to fashion.

HANDS OFF OUR HIJAB

You will come across Muslim women who hold some strange views like it's okay to be queer, or when women are on their periods, it's okay to fast, and their favourite one is, 'Hijab isn't fard (obligatory), it's your choice.' These women are very loud online. They write books like 'It's Not About the Burqa' and 'You Must be Layla'; others have PhDs in Islamic Theology and big bookstagram accounts. So should we listen to the anti-hijab squad?

Let's cut to the chase and call a spade a spade. The anti-hijab squad are mainly progressive Muslims who want to change Islam. Progressive Muslims identify as Muslims but discard Islam's fundamental practices because they disagree with their personal views and choices. They are a brand of Muslims who say there are alternative rules even though we have 1400 years of scholarly consensus and firm evidence from the Qur'an and Prophetic traditions for the rules.

In addition to their blatant dislike of the hijab, they are pro-LGBTQIA+, promote interfaith marriages and claim that women can lead mixed con-gregational prayers. Here are just a few examples of public statements made by progressives: 'I think Shariah [law] is totally made up. "It's not like there's a page in the Qur'an that says, 'For you to be Muslim, you have to live by these set of rules.' Ani Zonneveld, Muslims for Progressive Values.[67]

'Today, in the 21st century, most mosques around the world, including in the United States, deny us, as Muslim women, our Islamic right to pray without a headscarf,' Asra Nomani, Nomani co-founder of the Muslim Reform Movement. Nomani, a self-proclaimed Muslim reformer, has openly supported policies targeting Muslims due to their religious identity. In 2012, Nomani stated she was 'relieved that our country's largest police agency was monitoring our Muslim community'[68]

Moreover, radical feminists and self-appointed saviours like the Egyptian-American writer Mona Eltahawy believe Muslims need a sexual revolution. Ironically, Eltahawy accomplishes the very thing she accuses Islamic patriarchy of denigrating the choices of Muslim women. 'I support banning the face veil everywhere and not just in France, where they are to vote on a resolution and possibly a ban on wearing the garment in public places...'[69]

A further example is that of Amina Wadud, an American professor and proponent of Islamic feminism: 'I have recognised and lived the idea that hijab is a public declaration of identity with Islamic ideology. I do not consider it a religious obligation, nor do I ascribe to it any religious significance or moral value per se. It is certainly not the penultimate denotation of modesty.'[70] Wadud has also openly advocated 'pluralism' and 'equality' as an endorsement of LGBTQ+ rights.

In a newspaper article Hafsa Lodi asserts, 'Shariah is continuously open to revision, according to numerous religious scholars.'[71] The question arises as to why Lodi, a journalist supposed to be unbiased, only references the works of liberal progressive authors and activists such as Mustafa Akyol, Abdullahi Ahmed An-Na'im, Leila Ahmed, Ziba Mir Hosseini and Amina Wadud.

She disregards the views of mainstream Muslim scholars or academics, a tactic used all too often by non-Muslim journalists eager to find so-called independent voices in Muslim academia. This support reveals an attempt to undermine Islamic practices and take advantage of the general igno-rance of Islamic legal principles to advance an anti-hijab position. Many governments support such narratives in the west as part and parcel of an agenda to reform Islam.

So should we listen to the opinions of progressive Muslims regarding hijab? Are they practising Islam correctly? Yasir Qadhi, the dean of aca-demic affairs at Al-Maghrib Institute, points out, 'The very fact that the movement is so small or marginal speaks volumes about their sway and influence,' says Qadhi, 'Let's look at the text of the Qur'an and see what Allah and his messenger want us to do rather than to project our ideas onto the text.'

InshaAllah, I will now explain the scholarly, mainstream Islamic opin-ions regarding the hijab. Consensus has always existed amongst the sa-haba (companions of the Prophet) and classical scholars that wearing a headcover (khimar) and loose outer garment (jilbab) is obligatory. It is only in recent times that the rules of hijab has come under scrutiny as attempts to recast Islam in a liberal image. The following are primary evidences from the Quran and Sunnah regarding the compulsory nature of the hijab, as mentioned in the following verse:

'And tell the believing women to reduce [some] of their vision and guard their private parts and not expose their adornment except for what is apparent and let them draw their headcovers over their chests and not expose their adornment except to their husbands, their fathers, their hus-bands' fathers, their sons, their husbands' sons, their brothers, their brothers' sons, their sisters' sons, their women, that which their right hands possess, or those male attendants having no physical desire, or

children who are not yet aware of the private aspects of women. And let them not stamp their feet to make known what they conceal of their adornment. And turn to Allah in repentance, all of you, O believers, that you might succeed.' (Surah Nur 24:31)

Let's try to understand this verse and what it is asking us to do. Ibn Kathir, in his tafsir, said, 'It is possible that Ibn Abbas and those who followed him intended by the explanation of the verse, *'Except for what is apparent,' (24:31)* to mean the face and the hands, and this is the well-known opinion among the majority.'

Urwah reported: Aisha, said, *'May Allah have mercy on the foremost women of the Muhajirun. When Allah revealed the verse, 'let them draw their head covers over their chests' (24:31), they cut their sheets and veiled themselves with them.' (Bukhari)*

Aisha reported: Asma' bint Abi Bakr entered the house of the Messenger of Allah (saw) while she was wearing a thin garment, and she showed it to him. The Prophet said, *'O Asma, when a woman reaches the age of maturity, it is not proper for her to show anything but this and this,' and the Prophet pointed to his face and hands. Sunan Abī Dāwūd.*

The following verse is in relation to the command of wearing loose outer garments: *'O Prophet, tell your wives and your daughters and the women of the believers to bring down over themselves their outer garments. That is more suitable that they will be known and not be abused. And ever is Allah Forgiving and Merciful.' (Surah Ahzab 33:59)*

The meaning of 'To bring down over themselves their outer garments '(jalabeeb)' indicates that women should cast their outer garments over their persons. To lower the covering means to let it drape down. The jilbab is a cover (milhafah) used to conceal a dress and other items of clothing. It is stated in the al-Qamus al-Muheet (The Arabic Dictionary *Al-Qāmūs al-Muḥīṭ* was compiled by Muḥammad b. Ya'qūb al-Fayrūzābādī (d. 817 AH) that the jilbab is in the form of the (sirdāb) or the (sinmār), which is the gown or a loose garment for women, or that which conceals her clothing like a cover (milhafah). Al-Jawhari stated in as-Sihah (another dictionary) that the jilbab is the cover (milhafah), and some say it is a sheet (mulā'ah). There are differences amongst the ulema about the length of the jilbab and how far should it 'drape' but not about the necessity of a loose-fitted outer garment when a woman is in public.

It has been narrated on the authority of Umm Atiyyah (ra): *'We were ordered to bring out our menstruating women and veiled women in the religious gatherings and invocation of Muslims on the two 'Eid festivals. These menstruating women were to keep away from prayer, witnessing the blessing and call to the Muslims. I asked: 'Oh, Messenger of Allah! What if one of us does not have a jilbab?' He said, 'Let her wear the jilbab of her sister.'* (Muslim)

This means that she did not have a garment to wear over her clothes to go out in, so the Prophet (saw) ordered her to borrow one from her sister. The verse clarifies that Allah has commanded the Prophet (saw) to tell his wives and the wives and daughters of the Muslims to loosen their garments worn over their clothes which drape down.

The obligatory nature of the Islamic dress code has been confirmed by the statements of the men and women at the time of the Prophet (saw) and by centuries of scholarship, from Imam Nawawi, Ibn Manzur, and Ibn Hazm, to contemporary scholars, including Dr Haifaa Younis, Sheikh Nuh Keller, Sheikh Faraz Rabbani, Ustadha Maryam Amir, Shaykh Mohammad Akram Nadwi, Dr Shadee Elmasry, Ustadha Fatima Barkatulla and Imam Omar Suleiman.

InshaAllah, I will now present a series of arguments countering the views against wearing the hijab.

1. The Arabic word 'hijab' is not mentioned in surah 24:31. The term 'hijab' means a screen, not a headcover. Therefore, women do not have to wear hijab.

Allah says in the Quran: *'And when you ask (his wives) for anything you want, ask them from behind a screen (hijab).' (Al Ahzab: 53).* It's true in the Quran that the word hijab does not mean headcover. The literal meaning of the word hijab in Arabic is a curtain. It also means hiding, obstructing and isolating someone or something. In the past, the Arabs did not use the word hijab when referring to the headcover. In modern times it has become synonymous with headcover, and we all use it now. So it is correct to say it was never historically used to describe the cloth to cover the hair.

So how do we know we have to cover our heads? Allah says: *'And let them draw their head-coverings (khumur) over their necks and chest (juyoob).' (An-Nur: 31)* Khumur is the plural of khimar, and it is used to cover the head. Juyoob is the plural of jayb. It is the v-neck opening of a garment, often translated as bosom but encompassing the chest and collarbone area. Thus, Allah (swt) ordered that the khimar be worn over the head and around the neck and chest. So, Allah uses 'khimar' in the Quran, not hijab, to instruct us to cover our heads. The khimar is, in other words, what we now describe as 'hijab'.

2. The word used in surah 24:31 is 'khimar', but that is open to interpretation. It does not mean headcover. The term 'khimar' means shawl. So how do we know khimar is a headcover?

The root word of khimar is kha ma ra: to cover. Khamr (wine) is called such because it covers the human intellect. In the first Arabic dictionary written in 170 H by al-Khalil Ibn Ahmad, there we can find the term *Mukhammarah* which means goat or sheep, specifically a that has a white head. It is said that it is a black goat with a white head. The word khimar linguistically means a covering of the head. It was used to describe such a covering before Islam, and the word has been used to describe the head covering of men. It was one of the names for their turban if it was extra-long and went down to the middle of the belly.

Umm Salamah reported that: The Prophet used to wipe over the shoes and khimar. (Muslim) Ibn Manzoor comments: she meant the 'turban' because a man covers his head with it as a woman does the same by her khimar. It is reported that when one of the daughters of the Prophet (saw) died, he was handing them the clothes to wrap her. The hadith says: *'Then he gave us the Der'a (shirt) followed by the khimar (head cover) then the malhafah (The last piece to wrap the entire body)' (Ahmad & Abu Dawood)*

The Prophet (saw) said: *'Allah does not accept the prayer of any woman who menstruates unless (she wears) a khimar (head cover).' (Ibn Majaah)*[What is meant by a 'woman who menstruates' here is a woman who has reached the age of menstruation, not a woman who has her menses.]

A pre-Islamic style of head covering worn by women was a long cloth tied like a bandana, and then the remaining material would be draped behind their backs. That was also called a khimar. The Quran instructed women to take their khimar and throw it in front of them over their chests. *'And let them draw their head-coverings (khumur) over their necks and v-necks (juyoob).' (An-Nur: 31)*

The words and sentences of the Qur'an are interpreted according to their linguistic and shariah meanings Thus, it is incorrect to interpret them in any other way. Only a qualified scholar of the Quran, man or woman, can interpret and explain the meaning of ayat. But even they are bound by the linguistic definitions of the words, as the Qur'an was revealed in Arabic.

A layperson cannot take the words of the Qur'an and attempt to translate them in a way that contradicts the precise linguistic meanings of terms, let alone build an argument based on English translations. Samina Ali did this in her TEDx talk, *What does the Quran really say about a Muslim woman's hijab?* She attempted to argue that the word 'khimar' simply means to cover and not to cover the head, which, as I have explained above, is not accurate.

The question, then, is why didn't Allah (swt) explicitly mention the words' hair' or 'head' in the ayah? This is precisely why claiming the word simply means 'cover' is problematic. The word khimar describes a specific type of cover, the one that covers the hair. In the same way, a 'sock' in the English language is known to be a cover for the feet.

Here are just a few of the skills and knowledge a person must have before they can derive a ruling from an ayah of the Qur'an a person must know:

1. Classical Arabic linguistics, which is the language of the Quran.

2. The fundamental rules concerning the principles of the theory of Islamic law.

3. Knowledge of the Quran methodology in permission, prohibition, obligation and enforcement.

4. The hadith related to that issue.

5. Consideration of the linguistic meaning and the various contexts where a word was mentioned.

Deriving rules from the Quran and sunnah is a specialism and requires years of study like any other specialism. Taking one English translation of an ayah in isolation and ignoring all the other ayat and hadith relating to a topic is a misleading and deceitful method of deriving an Islamic rule.

3. Male scholars have interpreted the ayah and hadith about the hijab. Their interpretations are outdated, and we need women to interpret them instead in the modern context.

The myth that Muslim men have conspired to silence the voices of Muslim women needs to be discussed. Firstly, the gender of a hadith narrator or scholar is irrelevant. Secondly, to disprove the myth, the majority of the evidences related to women covering was narrated by female sahabi such as Aisha (ra) the wife of the Prophet, Zainab (ra), Umm Salama (ra), and they are the ones who conveyed how women interpreted the ayah and hadith in their daily actions. We are not obeying men or male scholars when we cover; we are obeying Allah. Here are just a few examples.

Allah reveals the verse for women to veil. Urwah reported: Aisha, may Allah be pleased with her, said, *'May Allah have mercy on the foremost women of the Muhajirun. When Allah revealed the verse, 'Let them draw their cloaks over their bodies,' (24:31) they cut their sheets and veiled themselves with them." Source: Ṣaḥīḥ al-Bukhāri*

Muslim women should only reveal their face and hands in front of non-mahram men. Aisha reported: Asma' bint Abi Bakr entered the house of the Messenger of Allah (saw) while she was wearing a thin garment, and she showed it to him. The Prophet said, *'O Asma, when a woman reaches the age of maturity, it is not proper for her to show anything but this and this,'* and the Prophet pointed to his face and hands. Also, throughout Islamic history, female companions and female scholars were all active in the field of gaining knowledge and teaching it to men and women.

The book al-Muhaddithat: the women scholars in Islam by Mohammad Akram Nadwi, illustrates this point. This book is an adaptation in English of the introductory volume of a 40-volume biographical dictionary (in Arabic) of women scholars of the Prophet's hadith. Learned women enjoyed high public standing and authority in the formative years of Islam. For centuries after that, women travelled intensively for religious knowledge and routinely attended the most prestigious mosques and madrasas across the Islamic world. Typical documents (like class registers and ijazahs from women authorising men to teach) and glowing testimonies about their women teachers from the most revered ulema are cited in detail.

Historically, women played a pivotal role in the foundation of many Islamic educational institutions:

- Fatima al-Fihri's founding of the University of Al Karaouine in 859 CE.
- Many female jurists existed. Fatima bint Alauddin al-Samarkhandi (d. 587 AH) was a jurist.
- Dr Faridah Zamarrud a female scholar of Tafsir/ Morocco.
- Zayn al-Nisa` bint 'Alamkir (1048-1113 h). She was the daughter of king Alamkir of India and had a complete tafsir of the Qur'an called Zayn al-Tafasir.
- Dr Aisha Abdul Rahman (Bint Al-Shati) wrote a tafsir.

Saying that women had never interpreted the Quran does not reflect a thorough or honest study of Islamic literature. Lastly, the point about juristic interpretation is that it's a discipline to seek Allah's verdict upon a matter without preconceptions. A scholar would be found out in the well-established Islamic process of 'peer review' if he was found to be deducing rules to confirm pre-determined biases.

4. Islam is outdated and must be modernised

One of the most cliched criticisms against Islam is that rulings revealed hundreds of years ago can have little impact on our lives in the 21st century. This has to be addressed. Wearing the khimar is a religious duty and a means of ibadat. Like all ibadat, it is aimed at worshipping and revering our Creator. Worship does not change through time and place. We wouldn't argue that salah, fasting, and charity need reforming, so why do we claim hijab does?

MUSLIM MISREPRESENTATION

Wanting to see teenagers who look like you portrayed positively in the media is normal. Popular culture, or pop culture as it is commonly known, is the term used to describe the dominant customs and elements of material culture in a specific society. The phrase defines cultural products (film, music, art, television, and books) that most people frequently consume.

I don't think it's unreasonable to want to see a female Muslim character with a loving, supportive family. Or a young woman converting to Islam and having a positive experience. Something is very wrong with pop culture when it comes to Muslims. Why are there no shows where a Muslim teen becomes stronger in their faith after hardship. Who doesn't want to whip off their hijab and jump into bed with a non-Muslim boy? Who rejects the hedonistic LGBTQIA+ lifestyle.

All I can say is don't hold your breath. Since their inception, Hollywood, Bollywood, Netflix, BBC and Channel 4 consistently create unrealistic tropes about teenage Muslimahs. Long story short, they have an image of what they want you to be, and then they create content that fits in with their vision of an 'ideal Muslimah'. Do they bother to ask Muslim girls what they want? No! But don't let their prejudice get you down. Instead, let's laugh at the top four cringe-worthy shows and movies that misrepresent Muslimahs.

Elite

The Netflix show Elite is an epic fail. The failure comes from the show presenting a Muslim girl taking off her hijab for a racist non-Muslim guy and her drug-dealing gay brother's dilemma with his faith. If this isn't the most random unrealistic plot ever, then I don't know what is.

The hijabi, Nadia, starts as a timid new girl at school who only studies and doesn't want to be friends with anyone. Unsurprisingly, the writers have intentionally included the stereotype of all hijabis being quiet and not speaking for themselves.

Nadia accidentally spots two of the show characters having sex, leading them to bet with each other to see if the non-Muslim boy, Guzman, can shame Nadia by seducing her. Plot twist, they both end up having feelings for each other, and Nadia becomes an independent, empowered woman who no longer follows her religion but does follow Guzman into his bed. Can you believe the show tweeted the scene where she took off her hijab and captioned it with 'QUEEN'.

This is such a cliched theme in almost every hijabi's storyline; there is practically no point in putting a Muslimah in a movie or TV show because it ends with an inaccurate representation and the Muslim girl being saved by a non-Muslim guy as a happy ending.

Things are no better for Omar, Nadia's brother, a homosexual drug dealer who falls in love with a male character in the show. I suspect the reason Elite made Omar homosexual was to persuade the Muslim audience that the LGBTQIA+ lifestyle is normal and 'love is love'.

Most Muslims consider these characters disrespectful to all Muslim teenagers. The show subtly implies to the audience that Islam goes against any teens' desires, making them miserable and leaving them with no choices.

It's no surprise to learn the writers of Elite are Spanish men and a trans woman. So none of the writers are Muslim, but they have used preexisting stereotypes they had in mind while shaping these characters and didn't even think about asking a Muslim to clarify what's right and wrong. It's a fairly safe bet that the creators of Elite are trying to convey that all Muslim teenagers must rebel against their strict religion and strict parents to be free and happy.

Hala

The movie follows a Muslim teenager struggling to balance desire with her familial, cultural and religious obligations. Her challenges immediately appear as parents versus classmates, America versus Pakistan, Islamic principles versus sexual freedom. Hala skateboards to school and writes poetry. She also clashes with her uncompromising parents, who criticise her relentlessly.

The audience is left with the impression that Hala must leave behind her parents, home, and hijab to live a meaningful life. Minhal Baig, the young American Pakistani director (I'm not sure if she is Muslim, nowhere online did it say she was), had a very clear vision for the movie 'I want young women to be able to watch the movie and really feel like, oh, that is me, and I am a sexual being. And I have my own sexual agency. And masturbating and having sex, those are things that young Muslim women do.'[72]

I know a minority of Muslimahs commit zina (premarital sex). But why is it that Baig and executive producer Jada Pinket Smith (in case you didn't know, she wore a scarf in a photo, and Muslims got happy) chose to create a movie about a Muslim teenager committing haram sex acts? In one scene, she tries to sleep with her English teacher. Really? These are the only realities portrayed over and over again. They are dishonest and harmful, with no attempt to represent the experience of the majority.

In an interview with Variety, Smith said she wanted Minhal Baig's 'voice to be heard and her story told.'[73] She endeavours to 'create inclusivity' 'where I have the power to.' It seems non-Muslims will only assist Muslim directors, writers, actors etc., who are the same as them: secular and liberal.

Amongst Muslim women, the reception to the movie has been resoundingly unfavourable. 'I am sorry, but the movie only portrays the same offensive stereotype of Muslim girls being oppressed by their parents and religion. I have never been identified with any Muslim-hijabi girl that has ever appeared in a movie or show because of this. We want to be portrayed as strong, independent women because that is what we are, not as victims of our own religion who need to be saved by an occidental non-Muslim guy.'[74]

'To think they could have made a movie many hijabis could relate to. This movie is horrible and promotes more hate to Islam. To see a girl that loves skating and writing. I could almost see myself in her. Until they showed she began to go away from her religion made me upset. The strong faith is the one that can get you through anything. This doesn't represent me as a young Muslim girl, and I can say it definitely does not represent Islam.'[75]

Everybody's Talking About Jamie

Jamie, a gay boy, lives with his single mother and secretly dreams of being a drag queen on stage. At school, Jamie confesses his desire to be a drag queen to his best friend Pritti Pasha - a girl constantly harassed for being Muslim. After the class bully insults Jamie and Pritti for being different, Jamie stands up for Pritti. Pritti returns the favour by encouraging Jamie to attend the school prom in drag. Pritti embraces all things LGBTQIA+. She is Jamie's biggest ally and cheerleader throughout the movie. As a Muslim, her behaviour is paradoxical: it makes no sense. I don't know any Muslim girl who would do what this character does.

Can a Muslim be an ally to the LGBTQIA+ community?

Should we uplift classmates who disobey Allah? Would you encourage your friends to commit zina? It would be easy enough to retort, but Islam emphasises loving people more than chastising them. The LGBTQIA+ community face discrimination, and we should help them. But in truth, Allah tells us in the Quran homosexuality is a grave sin, and he punishes people who act upon same-sex attraction:

'And (remember) Lut! When he said to his people, 'Do you commit Al-Fahishah (evil, great sin, every kind of unlawful sexual intercourse, sodomy) while you see (one another doing evil without any screen)? (Al-Naml 27:54-55)

In case you didn't know, Lut (as) wife was an ally to homosexual men. Allah destroyed Qawm Lut, and the angels informed Lut (as) that his wife *'will certainly suffer the fate of the others.' (Hud, 11:81)* So why would we want to follow in her footsteps? If we genuinely care about our friends, we would explain how Allah created men and women to be attracted to each other and provided the institution of marriage to

196

fulfil our need for love and intimacy. So, although the movie blatantly wants young Muslimahs to accept the Qawm Lut agenda, we know it goes against our beliefs. My bar for what constitutes 'indoctrination' is relatively high, but 'Everybody Loves Jamie' fits the bill.

Ms Marvel

At face value, how can you not love the idea of a teenage Muslim super-hero? I believe that shows like Ms Marvel presents a palatable Bolly-wood version of Islam that is non-threatening, politically neutral and de-void of religious integrity. Disney is under pressure to provide more posi-tive images of Muslims, but they will never consent to a favourable pic-ture of Islam.

Of course, this isn't an Islamic show. It's a superhero show where the main character is a Pakistani Muslim. So it's no surprise that Kamala has not one but three love interests. A black magic storyline is included about Jinn. And it's evident that a non-Muslim styled the hijabi characters' scarves because they rarely wear hijab correctly. In an interview, Sana Amanat, the co-creator of Ms Marvel said,

'I think that's why it was incredibly important to me for Nakia to be a hijabi but also very modern, someone who loves fashion, very much a feminist'[76]

The show does illustrate the experience of first-generation children born to immigrant parents with more cultural values than Islamic ones. The acceptance of not wearing hijab but prohibiting fitted clothing is an expe-rience for many girls. Immigrant parents not wanting their children to be too religious like the father says to the son. We've seen that. Aunties remarking on height and weight, gossiping about others' daughters, and marriage is the only thing to live for - these are all realities we see today.

But why are we rarely afforded the nuance and care that other cultures are? Confident Islamically-minded Muslimahs are excluded from writer's rooms where our stories can be heard, and our voices can make a difference. There's no doubt that Disney doesn't care about Muslims, and Ms Marvel is capitalising on the Muslim market.

Muslim writers, actors and directors assert, 'No group should be painted with one brush. Islam is a pluralistic faith, and I strongly believe that we are not a monolith. We have different people embracing different ways to express their faith, and we wanted the show to be able to encompass that.'[77]

They say teenage Muslimahs fall in love with non-Muslim guys, dance at weddings, go to parties and don't wear hijab; we must be authentic in our representation. But then they do not include a well-rounded female Muslim character who is happy to obey her creator when she faces challenges in her life and doesn't feel the need to commit haram openly.

So as much as we need positive Muslim representation in mainstream entertainment, Muslims equally should create their own media that proudly represent our beliefs and values and is not constrained by the constantly shifting value standards of others. To escape this trap, we should not seek approval or validation from non-Muslims by compromising our beliefs. As Allah says, *'And never will the Jews or the Christians approve of you until you follow their religion.' (Al-Baqarah, 2:120)*

MENTAL HEALTH
& DUA

Your emotional, psychological, and social well-being contribute to your mental health. It has an impact on how you think, feel, and act. Having positive mental health allows you to:

- Make meaningful contributions to your family and community
- Realise your full potential
- Cope with the stresses of life

Common mental health problems include:

- Anxiety or panic when you get so worried about things that it gets in the way of your life. Panic feels like you can't cope and are overwhelmed by fear.

- PTSD is when you have a deeply frightening experience, and it doesn't fade with time.

- Depression is when you feel down or more for more than a couple of weeks, and nothing makes you feel better. You can find it difficult to be bothered to do anything.

- Eating disorders when eating too much or too little becomes a problem for your health.

- OCD is when you have distressing thoughts, images or feelings and need everything to be done in a certain way so you feel better or 'just right' again.

Recognising mental health issues early can help to stop them from getting worse, but it's never too late to ask for support. The Prophet (saw) taught us to be proactive in life. One of my favourite hadith narrated by al-Tirmidhi describes how a man was leaving his camel without tying it. The Prophet (saw) asked him, *'Why don't you tie down your camel?' The man answered, 'I put my trust in Allah.' The Prophet (saw) replied, 'Tie your camel first, and then put your trust in Allah.'*

So if you need help or are worried about anything I mentioned in the book, please do something about it. Speak to your parents and family. Inshallah, they will find a way to help you. Everyone needs some extra support sometimes.

Another immediate action you can take to help yourself is to make dua to Allah. Dua is the first step to making sense of any problem. As Allah says, *'And it is Allah's Will to lighten your burdens, for humankind was created weak.' (An-Nisa, 4:28)*

Get into the habit of making dua regularly. We all know the power and importance of prayers, but sometimes we forget. For those of us living in societies such as the US and the UK, it's evident that religion plays only a cameo role. It's pushed to the periphery of life and makes a brief appearance during christenings, weddings, and funerals.

Unconsciously this mindset influences our thinking when it comes to making dua. Over time, in liberal states, a societal shift occurred; the role of religion is accepted but as a benign instrument, not as a guide in all walks of life. We feel the cultural consequences of that shift, so we sometimes forget to make dua.

How are we taught to solve our problems? By focusing on the supremacy of our individual talents and limitless potential. We are told to believe in ourselves and rely on our brainpower, skills, and knowledge. 'You can do anything you set your mind to!' To rely on God is backward, old-fashioned, and unscientific. Unwittingly, we absorb these unrealistic ideas from popular culture and social media. But these empty slogans ignore our need for divine guidance.

Allah created us with two undeniable attributes: human fitrah and a mind to comprehend His existence. We have an inbuilt disposition to search for and recognise the Creator. We are not independent, self-sufficient beings. We need our Creator's help. We are weak and needy. Without water or warmth from the sun, we would be dead in approximately three to four days. We cannot cause rain to fall or the sun to rise.

Like Prophet Ibrahim (as), we search for the perfect Creator of the sun, moon, and stars. Alhamdullilah, through the Quran and Sunnah, Allah has blessed us with a system to sanctify Him. An essential part of that system is dua. Remember, you will never find perfection in yourself, nor can you solve your problems alone. Navigating the swinging pendulum of life's highs and lows is no easy task. Utilise the most effective tool at your disposal, the best weapon in your arsenal: dua.

Let's remind ourselves of why dua is so powerful. Your Lord has proclaimed: *'Call upon Me, I will respond to you. Surely those who are too proud to worship Me will enter Hell, fully humbled.' (Ghafir, 40:60).*

Abu Hurairah narrated that the Prophet (saw) said, 'There is nothing more noble in the sight of Allah than dua' (Tirmidhi and Imam Ibn Majah).

When you make dua, you display the utmost humbleness and accept that no one can help you except Allah. Therefore dua is the essence of worship. Allah declares in the Quran: Say (O Muhammad): *'My Lord pays attention to you only because of your dua to Him. But now you have indeed denied (Him). So the torment will be yours forever (inseparable permanent punishment).' (Al Furqan, 25:77)*

In his tafsir of the above ayah, Qurtabi writes that Allah is telling us: 'I have not created you because I have need for you, I have only created you so that you may ask Me, so I will forgive you and give you what you ask.'

The Prophet (saw) said: *'Your Lord, may He be blessed and exalted, is characterised by modesty and generosity, and He is so kind to His slave that, if His slave raises his hands to Him, He does not let him take them back empty.'* (Abu Dawood)

In addition to Allah being Al-Mujeeb, He is also known as, Al-'Aleem (The All-Knowing), As-Samee' (The All-Hearing),
Al-Baseer (The All-Seeing) Al-Qareeb (The Very Close & Near).

The following Hadith Qudsi illustrates the power and majesty of Allah:
'O, my slaves! If the first of you and the last of you, and the humans of you and the jinn of you were all to stand together in the same exact time and asked Me for something. And I were to give everyone what he or she requested, then that would not decrease nor diminish whatever I own and whatever I possess! Except what is decreased in the ocean when a needle is dipped into it.' (Muslim)

The etiquette of making dua

Here are some guidelines and recommendations we should follow when making dua.

Only Allah can answer your dua

You must fully believe that only Allah is capable of hearing your prayer and only Allah has the power to change your situation. The Quran mentions this fact in *(An Naml, 27:6)*:
'Who (else is there) that responds to the call of the one in distress when he calls out, and He removes evil (from him), and makes you inheritors of the earth? Is there any other God besides Allah? Little is it that you remember!'

Be mindful

When asking for a God-fearing husband, pray to Allah sincerely. Abu Hurairah narrated that the Prophet (saw) said, *'Make dua to Allah in a state that you are certain that your dua will be responded to, and know that Allah does not respond to a dua that originates from a negligent, inattentive heart.' (Tirmidhi)*

Be grateful

Thanking Allah for what He has given us increases His favours upon us. Allah says, *'If you are grateful, I will surely increase you [in favour].' (Ibrahim, 14:7)*

Be in a state of wudu

One etiquette of dua is that a person is in a state of wudu (ritual purity) while making dua. This is illustrated in the hadith of Abu Musa al-Ashari, in which he stated that the Prophet (saw) after the Battle of Hunayn, called for water, performed wudu, then raised his hands and said: *'O Allah! Forgive Ubayd ibn Amir!'*

Raise your hands

Abu Musa al-Ashaari narrated: *'The Prophet (saw) made a dua, and I saw him raise his hands until I could see the whiteness of his armpits.'*

Send blessings upon the Prophet (saw)

The Prophet (saw) said: *'Every dua is covered until (the person) prays upon the Prophet (saw).'* The dua is covered means that it is not raised up to Allah until the person making the dua accompanies it with the prayer upon the Prophet (saw). However, it seems this is not an essential condition since the Prophet (saw) himself did not practice this all the time.

Pray with humility and fear

We must show humility to our Creator and humble ourselves before Him while making dua. *'Call upon your Lord with humility and in secret. Verily, He does not like the aggressors.' (Al Araf, 7:55)*

Recite the names of Allah

Our love for Allah increases when we contemplate the meaning of Allah's names. The best way to appreciate the importance of these names is to use the appropriate one when making dua. When you feel worried and ask for peace of mind, use Allah's name as-Salam (The Perfection and Giver of Peace). When you need Allah's guidance to make a decision, invoke Allah's name al-Haadi (The Guide). If you are confused, recite Allah's name al-Wakeel (The Trustee, The Disposer of Affairs) to help you make the correct decision. When you ask for sustenance, use Allah's name al-Razzaq (the One who Provides) and al-Ghani (the One who Gives and does not require anything). Whatever you are asking for, there is a divine name that you can use in your dua.

From every single one of His creations from the beginning until the end of time, He chose you out of the masses to worship Him. Your heart would not melt upon His remembrance if you didn't matter. If your problems weren't important to Him, the King of kings would not come down to the lowest heaven every night to listen to you. Allah, the merciful, has got you, no matter how small you and your problems may seem.[78]

Inshallah, have sabr and may Allah answer all your duas and give you good in this life and the next. As I mentioned at the beginning of the book, Muslim teenagers face unique challenges. But you also have unique solutions. And dua is the best solution given to you by Allah. Inshallah, trust Allah and do dua whenever you make a mistake, feel anxious or sad. Alhamdulilah it works for me every time!

My dear young beautiful sister, know that there are pearls of wisdom in everything that passes, a lesson to learn to move on to the next phase of your life. It's a tough journey to Jannah; no one said it would be easy. When you reflect on your life so far, do you see how Allah's plan was perfect for you the whole time? Allah is your guide. Embrace the journey, be smart, learn the lessons, and most importantly…trust in Allah.

ABOUT THE AUTHOR

Farhat Amin is an author & host of the podcast, her books include Smart Teenage Muslimah, Smart Single Muslimah, Hands Off Our Hijab and Child Loss, Bereavement & Hope. She has delivered lectures & courses on Women in Islam and feminism. She shares life advice that is Islamic and honest thought-provoking via her website www.smartmuslima.com. Where you can enrol in her Pre-marriage Course For Muslims, and Sex Education for Muslimahs.

Her aim is to help women achieve confidence in their faith. The inspiration for both her website and podcast is Surah Asr:

"By Time. The human being is in loss. Except those who believe, and do good works, and encourage truth, and recommend patience."

She felt there was a need for a platform that represents Muslim women without falling into the temptation of watering down Islam for the sake of mass appeal. As Islam encourages hikmah (wisdom) when informing others of Islam, not compromise.

You can connect with Farhat by signing up to her newsletter via www.smartmuslima.com, following her on Instagram @farhatamin_uk or emailing hello@farhatamin.com.

GLOSSARY

Adultery - Sex between a married person and someone else who is not the person's spouse. Islam forbids adultery.

Anus - The opening between a person's buttocks where solid waste comes out. It is haram for a married couple or people of the same gender to have sex via the anus.

Agnostic - A person who believes it is impossible to know whether God exists.

Atheist - A person who does not believe that God or gods exist.

Body Image - How we think about ourselves physically and how we believe others see us.

Caliphate - An Islamic government, that comprehensively rules by Islam following the sunnah of the Prophet (saw). The elected head of state is called a Caliph. Currently, there is no Caliphate in the Muslim world. Most countries rule by a combination of laws taken from Islam and the colonial powers that once ruled them.

Capitalism - An economic system in which investment in and ownership of the means of production, distribution, and exchange of wealth is made and maintained chiefly by private individuals or corporations, especially as contrasted to cooperatively or state-owned means of wealth. The majority of secular liberal states in the west are capitalist. It's also called a free market economy.

Cervix - The narrow end at the opening of a woman's uterus.

Egg - A cell that is produced in the ovaries that can combine with a sperm to make a baby.

Ejaculation - The release of sperm from the penis.

Erection -The state in which a man's penis becomes firm.

Fallopian tubes - A pair of tubes that carry eggs from the ovaries to the uterus

Feminism - At its core, feminism is the belief in full social, economic, and political equality for women. Feminism largely arose in response to Western traditions that restricted the rights of women, but feminist thought has global manifestations and variations.

Fertilisation - The process of a sperm uniting with an egg to form a new living cell.

Fiqh - As a juristic term it has two meanings. Having knowledge of Shariah (Islamic law) rulings which are extracted from the legislative sources. And it can also refer to the entire body of Islamic law.

Fornication - Sexual intercourse between people who are not married to each other. This is haram.

Hadith - A record of the words, actions, and the silent approval of Prophet Muhammad (saw) as transmitted through chains of narrators. Ahadith were collected by famous Muhaddiths such as Imam Bukhari. They verified narrators via very stringent rules, i.e. if a narrator was known to be unreliable then it would not be taken from that person. Ahadith are a source of legislation for Muslims.

Humanist - A person who believes in humanism, a system of thought that considers that solving human problems with the help of reason is more important than religious beliefs.

Incel - is short for involuntary celibate. They can't get a sex life despite the fact that they want to be in a relationship. Discussions in incel forums are often characterised by misogyny, self-pity, racism, and the endorsement of violence against women.

Ijtihad - exhausting all ones effort in studying a problem thoroughly and seeking a solution for it from the sources of the Shariah (i.e. Quran, sunnah etc.).

Jilbab - A loose, long-sleeved, full-length overgarment worn by Muslim women when they go outside.

Ideology- The belief is that religion should not be involved with a country's social and political activities.

Individualism - The idea that freedom of thought & action for each person is the most important quality of a society, rather than shared effort and responsibility

Liberalism - A political and moral philosophy that emphasises individualism, equality of opportunity, and the protection of individual rights. Primarily to life, liberty, and property.

Mufassir - An author of a tafsir.

Mujtahid - A person who is capable of performing Ijtihad to derive rulings from their detailed Islamic evidences.

Naturalist - A person who studies animals, plants & other living things.

Ovaries - A pair of organs in a woman that produce eggs and female hormones.

Ovulation - The release of a mature egg from an ovary.

Paganism - A religion that worships many gods, Pagans follow a spiritual path that worships nature, the cycles of the season, and astronomical markers and goddesses. They make up the rules as they go along.

Patriarchy- Social organisation marked by the supremacy of the father in the clan or family, the legal dependence of wives and children, and the reckoning of descent and inheritance in the male line broadly : control by men of a dispropor-tionately large share of power.

Penis - The organ at the front of a man's body used for sex and releasing urine.

Physiological - relating to the way in which the bodies of living things work.

Popular Culture - Refers to the traditions & material culture of a particular soci-ety. In the West, pop culture refers to products such as music, art, literature, fashion, film and television consumed by most people.

Psychosis - a mental disorder that causes difficulty distinguishing between what is real and what is not. Symptoms may include delusions and hallucinations, incoherent speech, and inappropriate behaviour in a given situation.

Rational - Behaviour, ideas, etc. based on reason rather than emotions.

Rectum- The last part of the large intestine that helps digest food and stores sol-id waste.

Secular - Not pertaining to or connected with religion.

Secularism - The belief is that religion should not be involved with a country's social and political activities.

Self-objectification - when people view themselves as objects for use instead of as human beings. Self-objectification is a result of objectification, and common-ly discussed in the topic of sex & gender, most commonly seen among women.

Semen - A sticky, whitish liquid that contains sperm that is ejaculated through the penis.

Shariah - refers to the entire body of laws derived from the legislative sources of Islam: the Quran, the sunnah, Ijma al sahabah (consensus of the companions) and Qiyas (analogical deduction). These are the four sources in Islam most widely accepted by the Mujtahideen and scholars of Usul al fiqh[79]

Socialisation -The process beginning during childhood by which individuals acquire the values, habits, and attitudes of a society.

Sunnah - Those actions of the Prophet (saw), which he (saw) initiated, performed and promoted among all his followers, as a part of Allah's religion.

Tafsir - An explanation of the meaning of the Quran.

Testicles - A pair of male organs that produces sperm and male hormones

Transgender - The idea is that people should count as men or women according to how they feel and what they declare, instead of their biology.

Uterus - A muscular organ in a woman's body where a baby grows.

Wicca - A western pagan religion that worships God and Goddess, the deities can vary according to the tradition and group. Wicca is connected to nature and the cycle of the seasons. Magic, spells, and manifestations are all essential to Wicca.

Vagina - A muscular canal lined with nerves and mucus membranes. It connects the uterus and cervix to the outside of the body, allowing for menstruation, intercourse, and childbirth.When people talk about the vagina, they're usually referring to the vulva, which is the outer part of the female genitalia. The vulva includes the: labia, vaginal opening, clitoris and urethra.

Zygote - A fertilised egg. A single cell formed by the combination of an egg and sperm.

REFERENCES

1 @feedyourruh, Instagram account
2 https://sarahprout.com/about/
3 https://www.teenvogue.com/story/modern-paganism-witches
4 ibid
5 https://www.teenvogue.com/gallery/why-witchy-culture-is-now-taking-over-the-beauty-world
6 https://www.teenvogue.com/story/modern-paganism-witches
7 https://www.vogue.co.uk/beauty/article/witchtok
8 https://en.islamway.net/fatwa/56295/why-did-you-become-muslim
9 https://www.theguardian.com/technology/2021/sep/14/facebook-aware-instagram-harmful-effect-teenage-girls-leak-reveals
10 ibid
11 https://www.maybelline.com/collections/volum-express
12 https://www.asos.com/women/new-in/cat/?cid=27108
13 https://www.pewresearch.org/fact-tank/2019/07/12/a-growing-number-of-american-teenagers-particularly-girls-are-facing-depression/
14 Yasmin Mogahed. Reclaim Your Heart. FB Publishing. 2012, p. 55.
15 https://news.gallup.com/poll/353645/nearly-half-adults-tried-marijuana.aspx
16 https://www.kcl.ac.uk/news/high-potency-cannabis-linked-to-higher-rates-of-psychosis
17 https://www.psychologytoday.com/ie/blog/finding-new-home/202110/10-key-reasons-why-people-smoke-marijuana
18 https://www.theguardian.com/books/2015/jun/21/selfies-sex-body-image-teenage-girls-young-adult-fiction-louise-oneill-interview
19 https://muslimmatters.org/2020/08/17/drowning-in-bottles-my-muslim-story-of-addiction-and-substance-use-disorder/
20 https://www.theguardian.com/society/2022/may/12/sadiq-khan-launches-commission-to-examine-cannabis-legality
21 https://metro.co.uk/2019/06/26/traces-of-cocaine-found-throughout-houses-of-parliament-10075256/
22 @feedyourruh, Instagram account
23 https://www.theguardian.com/culture/2020/jan/31/porn-survey-uk-teenagers-viewing-habits-bbfc
24 https://www.psychologytoday.com/us/basics/dopamine
25 https://www.councilonrecovery.org/how-pornography-affects-the-teenage-brain-infograph/
26 https://www.forbes.com/sites/frankicookney/2019/10/20/porn-was-legalized-50-years-ago-this-is-how-the-business-has-changed/?sh=2b692851ec7e
27 https://www.nspcc.org.uk/keeping-children-safe/online-safety/inappropriate-explicit-content/online-porn/
28 https://www.theguardian.com/music/2021/dec/15/billie-eilish-says-watching-porn-gave-her-nightmares-and-destroyed-my-brain
29 https://www.nspcc.org.uk/
30 https://en.wikipedia.org/wiki/Feminist_views_on_pornography
31 https://www.standard.co.uk/esmagazine/jlo-interview-jennifer-lopez-hustlers-a4227651.html
32 https://www.bustle.com/articles/121088-zendaya-defines-feminist-in-a-way-that-will-make-you-want-to-shout-your-feminism-from
33 Imam Abu Bakr ibn Abi Shaybah, Imam Tabari and Imam Ibn Abi Hatim have recorded this statement of Sayyiduna 'Abdullah ibn 'Abbas (Musannaf Ibn Abi Shaybah, 19608, Tafsir Tabari and Tafsir Ibn Abi Hatim, Surah Al Baqarah, Verse: 228. Also see Tafsir Ibn Kathir)
34 https://muslimmatters.org/2010/10/04/muslimah%e2%80%99s-guide-to-puberty-how-to-talk-to-your-daughter-about-adolescence/
35 https://www.nhs.uk/conditions/gender-dysphoria/treatment/
36 https://www.bbc.co.uk/news/education-57411363
37 https://www.cage.ngo/casework
38 https://www.preventwatch.org/about/

39 @feedyourruh, Instagram account
40 https://islamqa.info/en/answers/5538/who-is-a-womans-mahram
41 https://www.pewresearch.org/fact-tank/2019/07/12/a-growing-number-of-american-teenagers-particularly-girls-are-facing-depression/
42 https://www.pewresearch.org/fact-tank/2019/02/26/the-concerns-and-challenges-of-being-a-u-s-teen-what-the-data-show/
43 https://www.theguardian.com/society/2009/sep/01/teenage-sexual-abuse-nspcc-report
44 https://worldpopulationreview.com/
45 ibid
46 https://www.cdc.gov/std/statistics/2021/
47 https://www.womenshealthmag.com/health/a19971397/caitlyn-jenner-transition-surgery/
48 https://thetranscenter.com/transwomen/
49 https://www.piratewires.com/p/transmaxxing?utm_source=%2Finbox&utm_medium=reader2
50 https://unherd.com/thepost/why-are-incels-turning-themselves-into-girls/
51 https://www.piratewires.com/p/transmaxxing?utm_source=%2Finbox&utm_medium=reader2
52 https://unherd.com/2023/01/how-we-created-a-self-hating-generation/
53 ibid
54 https://muslimmatters.org/2022/06/21/fatwa-regarding-transgenderism/
55 Helen Joyce. 'Trans'
56 https://www.dailymail.co.uk/news/article-6124077/Ninety-cent-sexual-assaults-public-swimming-pools-happen-unisex-changing-rooms.html
57 https://www.itv.com/news/anglia/2022-09-26/primark-reviews-unisex-changing-rooms-as-men-walk-in-on-woman
58 https://www.dailymail.co.uk/news/article-6124077/Ninety-cent-sexual-assaults-public-swimming-pools-happen-unisex-changing-rooms.html
59 https://www.theguardian.com/uk-news/2018/oct/11/transgender-prisoner-who-sexually-assaulted-inmates-jailed-for-life
60 https://fairplayforwomen.com/stonewalls-non-binary-demands-undermine-womens-protections/
61 https://muslimmatters.org/2022/06/21/fatwa-regarding-transgenderism/
62 https://www.prnewswire.co.uk/news-releases/islamic-clothing-market-size-worth-88-35-billion-by-2025-cagr-5-0-grand-view-research-inc--820570235.html
63 https://aminashareef.com/2020/09/04/warping-faith-big-brands-and-government-are-refashioning-muslim-identity/
64 https://www.arabnews.com/node/1768831/fashion
65 https://simplysociology.com/anomie-theory-sociology.html
66 https://qarawiyyinproject.co/2017/11/25/people-think-hijab-sexualises-young-girls-because-of-the-muslim-community/
67 www.huffpost.com/entry/progressive-muslims-launch-gay-friendly-women-led-mosques
68 www.thedailybeast.com/airport-security-lets-profile-muslims.
69 Mona Eltahawy, Is France Right to Ban the Burka in Public? www.guardian.com.
70 Amina Wadud, Page 220, Inside the Gender Jihad.
71 https://www.independent.co.uk/voices/taliban-sharia-law-muslim-feminist-women-b1905249.html
72 "Hala Director Minhal Baig On Making A Movie For First Generation Muslim-Americans". *MTV News*. Retrieved 2020-02-27
73 https://variety.com/video/jada-pinkett-smith-oscars-female-director-shut-out/
74 Sen Kuroba on Youtube
75 Salma posted on Youtube
76 https://www.amaliah.com/post/65429/ms-marvel-muslim-representation
77 ibid
78 @feedyourruh, Instagram account
79 , Iyad Hilal, Studies in Usual al Fiqh

Made in the USA
Las Vegas, NV
14 December 2024

14271887R00125